# MY GREATEST SOLO

# MY GREATEST SOLO

# Accompanied by Grace

*A Memoir of Faith, Motherhood, and the
Music Industry in Nashville*

**Dawn M. Delvo**

Published by Loved by Delvo Publishing LLC
Nashville, Tennessee

ISBN: 979-8-9959521-0-7

Manufactured in the United States of America

To my daughter, Evelyn May.

My mission goes beyond being a good mother to you. It is to share what Jesus has done in our story so that other women may find hope in their own story, already written, and choose God's plan with peace.

*"For I know the plans I have for you," declares the Lord,*
*"plans to prosper you and not to harm you,*
*plans to give you hope and a future."*
**– Jeremiah 29:11**

# WITH GRATITUDE

This book, and this life, would not have been possible without the support, leadership, and love I've received from my family at Black River Entertainment.

To Gordon and Kim Kerr, thank you for your generosity, creativity, unwavering encouragement, and for modeling what it means to live a faith-first life with purpose and integrity.

To Kim Pegula, thank you for your vision, your drive, and your faith.

To Terry and Kim Pegula, thank you for your extraordinary generosity and for helping make dreams possible for so many people, myself included.

# Table of Contents

# FOREWORD

I was born in Nashville, so this has always been my home. Some of my earliest memories are of the life my mom and I built together here. I remember the projects we did, baking, decorating, laughing, and jumping out from behind a corner to scare each other in our tiny loft apartment. I remember feeling happy and not ashamed that it was just my mom and me.

When things were uncertain, I noticed how calm she stayed. She was quiet and didn't try to freak me out, even when things were unknown. That made me feel safe.

As a kid, trusting God didn't look like having everything figured out. It looked like not worrying about the next step, waiting through Covid, waiting to buy a house, and trusting that things would work out when they were supposed to. I didn't always understand what was happening, but I knew we were okay.

One moment I felt really proud was when we got our house. It felt like something solid after a lot of waiting.

If I had to describe that season of our lives in one word, it would be blessed. We never had problems with food, bills, or having what we needed. Life wasn't perfect, but it was good.

Before you read this book, I want you to know this: Single parenting isn't always bad.

— Evelyn, Age 15

# THE BACK STORY



*SOLO – A performance in which the performer has no partner or associate: something undertaken or done alone.*

## The Seed

I don't know when I first knew that music was, and forever would be, a massive part of my life, but I knew I loved it and that music felt like home to me. It was like a divine magnet put in my heart to pull me towards my future—well, not my future, but the plan God had in store for my life. Luckily for me, most of my intentional plans never worked out.

Stephanie, my oldest sister, living at home while we were growing up, always had the biggest bedroom, and it was in the basement. There's a perceived coolness factor in having that room, and making it even more interesting was the attached storage room, the only other room on that level of our home in Bismarck, North Dakota.

In elementary school, that storage room was where my imagination ran wild. I'd spend hours stacking boxes and random boards across chairs to create a stage and set the right mood. Of course, no show is complete without glam, so I'd get all gussied up in concert clothes, makeup, and fake hair, often made of tinsel, and sing my heart out. I'd see Leonardo DiCaprio's face watching me from the *Romeo & Juliet* poster hanging on the nearby door and record into a single-speaker, gray karaoke machine. It had room for two cassettes, allowing me to record my voice over background music. I stayed up for hours singing, writing songs, and dreaming in that storage room.

A few years later, Stephanie graduated from high school and moved to the East Coast. It should have been Kristy's turn to have the basement room as the next oldest child, but she followed her own path down to Texas. That meant the downstairs was all mine, and I started high school with the "cool" basement bedroom. By then, I'd moved from my karaoke machine to a four-track recorder, a Christmas gift I was thrilled to receive from my parents. I remember feeling like a music chemist because when I'd connect the four-track to the karaoke machine and the karaoke machine to some speakers and then push "on," I'd always pray that nothing would blow up. Then I'd start singing and recording. I sang and sang and sang.

"Creak"

I heard a noise from the six stairs leading down to my painted black door. I was silently annoyed and waited for the footsteps to leave. My mom snuck up to my door to listen, but I was too embarrassed or self-conscious to let her in. That's weird, right? I've been going through all of this, and for what, if not for people to hear me?

All I can attribute it to is one night before Christmas in McClusky, ND. Grandma and Grandpa Tkach's house was always a safe place for my imagination to run wild and where dreaming was encouraged. Although we grew up Catholic, we went to Grandma and Grandpa's house for holidays and spent many nights before Christmas listening for reindeer paws on the slanted roof above the little blue room with two twin beds inside. I signed up to sing "Silent Night" in the Baptist church's Christmas concert that year. I was very young, and I remember going down the hall from the blue bedroom with a heart full of excitement. As I rounded the sharp corner to go down the long, fiery orange, shaggy carpeted staircase, I overheard the end of a conversation downstairs from a voice suspiciously similar to my mom's saying, "I just don't want her to embarrass herself."

Looking back, silly as it sounds now, that was the first time I ever doubted if I could make music. "Embarrass myself? Why would my singing in the Christmas service embarrass me? Or would I embarrass my family?"

Now, I'd give anything to have my mom sneak up on me to hear me singing.


*Grandma T*

My Grandma T has a way about her that makes everything unique for us. We always felt welcome and loved in her home. My first memories of learning about Jesus were in her Sunday School class in the basement level of the McClusky United Methodist Church, the sweet white church on the corner of Avenue C and Second St. E. in McClusky, ND. It was at Grandma and Grandpa's house that I had my first go at "baking," which, I'm sure, to the chagrin of my grandma, consisted of mixing flour and water to make "cakes" and "biscuits," which ultimately just resulted in a huge mess and would create a cement-like substance if not cleaned almost immediately. In that same basement, my grandma taught me about patience and grace as I learned how to sew on her vintage Singer sewing machine. What started in my breaking countless sewing needles while trying to make Barbie sleeping bags as a child resulted in my loving to sew as an adult. It's something I find a lot of peace in. Growing up, we knew we could count on an extraordinary 12 Days of Christmas tradition with our grandma. For each grandchild, she made a personalized 12-day bag with pockets that hold a gift for each of the 12 days counting down to Christmas. It was always exciting to receive the plastic grocery bags with our "12 Days" gifts each year. It was even more thrilling to try and guess what was in each parcel and reorganize them almost every day in anticipation of finding the "best" one. Because Grandma took the time to teach me how to sew, I was recently able to make the bags for her great-grandchildren on our side and continue that tradition.

When I wasn't "pouring concrete" or breaking sewing needles or trying desperately not to let a pool ball bounce off of the pool table in grandma's basement, I was seated at the black, time-worn, upright piano against the back wall to the left of the bathroom door plunking out notes. Grandma plays piano, but I rarely saw her play that one unless she was helping me. I don't know what made her think of doing this, but she bought little letter stickers and placed the corresponding note on every key on that board. Every time we made the trip to McClusky, I sat at that primarily out-of-tune piano and plunked out hymns, trying to learn a song or write my own. Every time, that is, until they chopped it up into little pieces because it was too big to remove from the basement intact. Sad right? That's a true story. Thankfully, my family saved pieces from the piano for us kids, and I have 10 of those precious keys, now mostly worn-out little letter stickers in a shadow box, hanging on the wall in my Nashville home.

*High School – Freshman Year*

I started high school with a white canvas. Schools in North Dakota are good, and I'd been in the public school system until the 9th grade. At that point, my parents and I decided that I'd go to Saint Mary's Central High School, a private Catholic school with an excellent music program. I knew a handful of students before attending, but the pages of my journals were about to be filled with new names and faces I'd never met. That said, many of the upperclassmen knew my name, or my last name, because of my older sisters.

I loved hearing "Little Delvo!" yelled in the hallway because it made me feel closer to my two sisters, who moved away and gave me an identity. Or a partial identity. That first year of high school, I made friends with four incredible and beautiful ladies. Jodi, Amy, Brita, and Mandi. Jodi is naturally beautiful, wise, innovative, and has bottomless dimples. (I love dimples). Amy is a spitfire who has an opinion and a daring spirit. She is brilliant, loyal, genuine, and someone I can talk to for hours. Brita is unnaturally beautiful, meaning ridiculously beautiful, and has a very kind heart. She drew people in, and I was one of them gratefully. Mandi is adorable, has dimples for days, and is a fun, goofy friend. Mandi and Jodi are cousins, so they have always known each other. Amy and Brita have gone to school with them their whole lives, so they are all tight. I was the outsider who was welcomed in, for the most part.

Freshman year was an interesting one. Between wanting to make friends, being known as "little Delvo," and trying to have fun, I sometimes found myself in compromising situations. North Dakota is beautiful, especially in the summer, but the winter is cold. I don't mean chilly, but let's go sledding anyway. But COLD, let's stay inside, go to someone's house, and play cards. (That means to drink.)

One night, my parents were out of town, and they trusted me to stay home alone. (Or I was permitted to be at a sleepover; that makes more sense thinking back.) Regardless, the plan was for us girls to have a slumber party and make margaritas. Not that we had a clue how to make them. My parents kept old and terrible liquor in the hall closet, and we mixed God knows what with ice and fruit. It was awful. Back in the day, on Friday nights, various schools played football games on the Hughes Junior High School field. There were two games, Junior Varsity and Varsity, and while we were bringing shame to the profession of mixology, I was about to bring shame to my name because, before the end of the Junior Varsity game, the word was out.

"Party at Delvo's!"

Because of that night, my house became the place to party that year, and there wasn't much respect for it since I was merely a freshman. People smoked in my home, binge drank alcohol, threw my mom's vinyl records like frisbees, and broke a countless number of them, not to mention other items in the house. One night in particular, it got so bad I called the cops myself to get people out of my house because I knew they would show up eventually. There was no control.

Thank God there were no Facebook, Twitter, or Instagram accounts back then. I can't imagine what it would have been like if there had been. Thinking about how much worse everything would have been is terrifying.

Because I attended a Catholic high school, we had religion class every year. My freshman year was interesting because I had a not-very-well-thought-out epiphany during a discussion on the difference between venial sins and mortal sins. Up on the chalkboard, there was a line between the two words and a list of examples under each. Venial sins: telling a lie, stealing, etc., and Mortal Sins: Murder, premarital sex, missing church...wait, what? At that moment, of comparing the classifications of sin, all I could think was, "Having premarital sex is just as bad as missing a church service? I've missed a lot of church; I could have had a lot of sex!" Now, thankfully, at that point in my life, I hadn't had sex, but it was a revelation I thought about often. Before graduating, I told my freshman religion teacher about that particular lesson, and he seemed very surprised by my interpretation. He said, "Dawn! That shouldn't have brought the weight of having sex down; it should have brought the weight of missing church up!" I thought, "Huh. Yeah, it didn't."

High school was a crucial turning point for me because of the choir program. St. Mary's Central High School was the first place to officially teach me that music was not only a creative outlet but was the first step towards the rest of my future in the music industry. That realization came to me well after I had graduated and moved far from home. My first real music industry job came from volunteering through the music program at school to usher the events that went to the Bismarck Civic Center through a contract with the venue and the school's music program. Through this volunteer opportunity, I was able to work/attend concerts by Garth Brooks, Wynonna, Newsboys, 3rd Day, KISS, and so many more. I usually ended up with the role of assisting with handicapped seating, which came with a walkie-talkie to aid communication, instantly making me feel important.

In addition to my first work experience in the music industry, SMCHS awarded me scholarships to attend the International Music Camp on the North Dakota/Canada border. I participated in this camp every summer for weeks at a time, and it was there that I learned who my people were. I found my place at this camp and felt comfortable, for the first time, with other music lovers. During these summers at IMC, I formed relationships that would forever influence my life. It was a priceless experience and one I recommend for any music-loving students who are up for it.

*High School – The Rest of It*

I set the tone for the rest of high school and the rest of my life that freshman year. That year came with many new faces, experiences, and turmoil. I didn't know it then, but God equipped me with the people, places, experiences, and direction I'd need throughout my adult life. The core friendships I made then still carry me through my days. The crushes I had then popped in and out of my life through college and on into my 30s.

My sophomore year was weird because I left town the summer before to live and work in Pick City, ND. My parents used to rent a cabin up there, which they ultimately purchased from our neighbors who owned it. We spent every summer I can remember in Pick City, playing on the lake and enjoying long sunny days with family and friends.

We spent days on end playing on the lakeshore, learning how to water ski, tubing behind our Sea Ray, and coming home starving to eat dinner with the family before having a bonfire and roasting marshmallows for s'mores. I wouldn't want it any different. It was always so fun to wake up and find out we were having company, too. Memorial Day, the 4th of July, my birthday, Labor Day, and any given weekend were open for visitors, and it was my favorite place on Earth.

That's also where I did a lot of work with my dad. Oh, Dad, lol. Sam Delvo is a character, and I love him very much. Some of my earliest memories of my dad revolve around popcorn and being his assistant for home improvement projects. Ha-ha, like the popular TV show, there were some issues from time to time. I once helped Dad sheetrock the ceiling. I'm 5'2 now if I'm lucky; imagine me at 12 years old, and he made some stand that if I kept it balanced, he could nail a full-sized sheet of sheetrock to the 8-10 ft ceiling. Unfortunately for my dad, I failed at that balancing act, and 100% dropped a sheet of sheetrock on my dad's head. He is a creative swearer in moments like those. Dad can string phrases together that I've never heard another human utter as a standard for him. At some point, I'd feel bad and usually cry, but for the most part, those experiences, painting, sheet rocking, shingling roofs, building a shed or a deck, or mowing lawns, were good bonding experiences with my dad. Those experiences also helped prepare me for life because I'm not afraid to try things, and I'm pretty handy.

Once, I got a flat tire, and after Ubering for two days, because it was amid a hectic work week, I set out to put the donut on myself and drive it somewhere to be fixed. Granted, one of my beautiful Australian neighbors jumped in to help me, but we knocked it out together once he had it on the jack. My point is that I'm not scared to work hard, get dirty, and give something my best shot, and I thank my dad for that tenacity.

In Pick City, I almost had another life. I had an entirely different job, friends, and routine. I had a boyfriend, and I had a lot of alone time. My first job up there was working for my now dear friend Fish at the bar/restaurant she owned with her then-husband. I started with dishes and backline prep, then some cooking (sorry to everyone who ate there), and became a waitress. I loved working there because I've always felt more comfortable around people who are older than me. That's still true now. That bar had a piano, and I would sit down at it and play music from time to time. Eventually, patrons would request that I sing a song, so I'd take breaks from serving to play a tune or two. After my shift, I'd have a ball if we had bands playing or karaoke nights.

Fish decided to sell the bar and then went to manage another place about 30 miles from my cabin, so the following summer, I worked there. The following summer, I worked at the Dam Bar across the street from Fish's old place. It's called the Dam Bar because Pick City, ND, is near Lake Sakakawea and the Garrison Dam. It's the damned-up Missouri River. Just thinking about this place takes me back and makes me miss it so much. I met Sara when I lived there, and we'd have "card night" in Riverdale. It was a great friend group; some worked for the US military, and some worked on farms, but we all had a blast together.

Every summer, we'd take an annual canoe trip from the Garrison Dam to Bismarck, ND. It would take us three days to canoe—I mean float—down the river, and it was an adventure I looked forward to every year. There are so many fun stories from those days—good, clean fun—but if I write about them, I may be admitting to breaking federal laws, so I'll have to talk about that in person sometime. Or not.

That is to say, my summers were jam-packed with self-discovery, growth, fun, and adventure. Returning to Bismarck and my friends in high school was a bit of a hard transition at times because I would disappear every year for a few months. I understand that more now than I did back then.

The most challenging transition was the first one, going into sophomore year. It was a little rough, and I also had more alone time than I anticipated in Bismarck. Often, I would feel uncomfortable eating lunches in the cafeteria, so I'd grab something and then go to a piano practice room and start figuring out how to play songs I liked on the piano. After a while, I began to write songs and finally put music to the songs I'd written but couldn't play. That time was invaluable because it solidified my passion for music, creating music, and performing music.

I can't go much further without talking about Vicky Boechler. Mrs. Boechler was my high school choir teacher. She's the one who encouraged me to challenge myself vocally. She is also the teacher who gave me that scholarship to the music camp I mentioned earlier. Saint Mary's had a vocal jazz program, and I was happily part of that group for three of my four years in high school. She was a good influence on me, even though we had some awkward or challenging moments. For example, the day she pulled me aside my freshman or sophomore year because she thought I was running with a "bad crowd." Or when I could not attend jazz choir auditions my junior year due to a family emergency that led to her offering me an "alternate position" in the vocal jazz group, which I declined. Each situation ultimately worked out for the best. We had some ups and downs, but thankfully, she was one of those significant influencers who encouraged and pushed me to be the best version of myself.

Thankfully, my girls stuck by me, and we had an excellent high school experience together.

Now, about the popcorn. Any of my friends from high school will tell you that Delvo popcorn is epic. My dad had this antique popper that goes on the stovetop, and you literally have to spin the handle the whole time it's cooking until it pops the top up. Once he'd finished the first of two batches, Dad put it in the big popcorn bowl and melted a few tablespoons of butter in the same popper. He'd pour the melted butter onto the still-hot popcorn, add salt, and then stir the batch by tossing the popcorn in the bowl like you would flip a pancake. It is so good.

*College Days*

I graduated from SMCHS in the year 2000. (I hear Conan O'Brien in my head. If you're around my age, you do too!) Post-graduation is another time when, honestly, I was just a passenger not paying attention to my life, and thankfully, God was driving the vehicle. My friends knew what they wanted to pursue after finishing school, and I had no idea. I thought about going to Berklee in Boston, MA, for a minute, but after going there for a visit, I never applied. It wasn't right for me. So, I was back in Pick City working at the bar. I don't remember hearing about Minnesota State University Moorhead, the small public university on the Minnesota/North Dakota border. Still, at some point, I applied and was accepted into their Music Business program.

In my freshman year at college, I lived with my friend Sara. She was one of my good friends from the lake, and we shared many summer adventures together. She was starting her senior year at NDSU in Fargo, ND and needed a new roommate to join her in the quaint brick quartet with hardwood floors and countless plants, near Main Street. Since Fargo/Moorehead are only separated by a river, it was easy for me to drive the couple of miles to school each day. I loved our little place and being her roommate.

The following year, God stepped into my life in one of the most significant ways I'd witnessed. Sara graduated and it was time for me to move out of the quartet and find a new place. Fargo was still pretty new to me, and I didn't know many people, so I ended up responding to a newspaper ad looking for a 3rd roommate to join the two girls already living there.

My dad and I drove to the white, two-story townhouse, the last in a string of townhouses across the street from the consistent whistle of a passing train, to meet my would-be roommates for the first time. I immediately liked the place when we stepped inside. It felt right after meeting Nikki and Jean; they agreed, and I moved in.

We wrapped up the summer with one of our legendary canoe trips on the Missouri River before I moved back to Moorhead, MN for school. During the excursion, I met my buddy's brother, and despite being warned not to, we started dating. Since he lived in Grand Forks, North Dakota, about an hour north of me once I returned to school, it seemed easy enough to keep going.

Then my world opened up. Things were going great with the boyfriend and in the townhouse. Not long into the semester, Angie, Amy, and so many more awesome people came into the picture. I was loving life and having fun. School? I don't know what was going on with school! Ha!

One morning early in the semester, I went to the bookstore to charge my books on my financial aid. As I was in the store, I felt uneasy, as if something was wrong, but I didn't know what the problem was. So, I went into self-preservation mode and made a beeline toward the exit. "I need to get somewhere safe," was all I kept thinking. As I passed the section with art supplies, I noticed that they all began to FLY. All around me, things were FLYING and FLOATING through the room.

"I need to get somewhere safe."

"I need to get somewhere safe."

The next thing I knew, I woke to hear an EMT say, *"You're okay. We're putting you in the ambulance."*

When I opened my eyes again, I saw a very scared Nikki. I don't know how they tracked down my new roommate, but she was at my side in the ER.

I later learned that I made it to the front of the bookstore before starting to teeter back and forth. I ultimately grabbed onto a bookshelf to steady myself before pulling it down on top of me as I fell to the ground, convulsing. I had had a seizure.

The hospital released me to my boyfriend, who was now living in Fargo, and he drove me to Jamestown, ND, the halfway point between my hometown and Moorehead, MN, to meet my dad. As we said our goodbyes, he said, "I love you." My dad was like, "What?" I was completely and utterly exhausted. I simply waved and said, 'Bye.' That conversation was the first time someone I was dating told me they loved me, and I was basically a zombie. The seizure zapped so much energy out of my body, and I could hardly process what he said to me. Once I was safely home and a little more rested in Bismarck, he called to check on me. At some point in the conversation, he said, 'I love you' to me for the second time. This time, I did process it, and it scared me. I wasn't ready to say that to him because I had never said it to a guy before. So, I answered him by saying, "That's so nice." Possibly the worst reply ever, but I wasn't expecting him to say that again. Looking back, I figure he was just scared.

I lost my license for six months because of the seizure and had to take the city bus. During that period, I spent a lot of time alone thinking and honestly became depressed. The meds I was on did not help that situation. What happened next truly blindsided me. Maybe it shouldn't have, and as I look back, I understand that God was entirely in charge. What I thought was one of the worst moments of my life was one of God's best-played hands.

Christmas was coming and as my boyfriend and I were driving back to my place, we saw a Christmas tree lot and decided to go buy one. Unfortunately, it was closed for the day, so we drove home in the dark, without a tree to lighten the mood.

To my surprise, the next day, he brought me my very own beautiful spruce tree, and we decorated it in my room. Gram bought us kids Christmas ornaments almost every year, so I had many great memories to share with him during the process. Afterward, we visited about Christmas gifts, and I asked him, "Since we're going to your grandparents' house, should I get them each a Christmas gift or just one for them as a couple?" He thought about it and replied, "Well, they are only getting you one, so one is good." Then he was quiet for a minute before saying, "I think we should break up." I laughed and said, "Yeah, me too." I thought he was joking. The dude just brought me a Christmas tree that we decorated together, and we are now discussing family Christmas gifts. He continued, "I think it's the best thing for us. You are going to move to Nashville and chase your dream…" His words started cutting, and I stopped hearing them.

Thankfully, he was kind and kept it short. That night, the tree came down, and when he returned the next day to give me back some of my things, he was welcomed with a very tinselly tree in the snowbank. No joke, seeing random strands of tinsel made me very angry for several years.

A lot changed after that. I discovered that my ex-boyfriend was now dating my friend, and I needed a fresh start. I moved into an apartment alone for the first time, which was perfect for me. Shortly after, she became pregnant with their son.

We had all moved on, but that's not where this triangle ends—quick backstory. I hate shopping. My poor mother was the victim of this hatred because I think she used the offer to go shopping as a way to bond with me, and I usually turned it down or had a terrible time in the store because I am not the person the trendy clothes are designed to fit. One particularly awful shopping experience with my mom was at JCPenney's in Bismarck, ND, my hometown. I heard an all-too-familiar voice call out my friend's name from a short distance away. When I looked in the direction of their voices, I saw my ex-boyfriend and my friend. I did what anyone would do in my situation; I jumped into the middle of the nearest circular metal clothes rack and hid in the coats. Thankfully, it was winter, so they provided excellent coverage. Sadly, I did not clue my mother into my drama, and as they neared our position, my mom yelled, "Dawn? Dawn, where are you?" I jumped out quickly, hoping they didn't see where I was bargain hunting. They were pushing their baby in a stroller, we had an awkward chat, and then they were gone.

When I return to that moment in my heart, I can still feel the pain, the betrayal, and the love. I cherish that period now because it showed me a peek at God's plan. I didn't realize it, but that breakup was a HUGE turning point for me. If he had asked me to marry him, I might have said "Yes." Instead, God said "No." to us and "Yes." to their now FOUR children, my beautiful daughter, and our dream life in Nashville. Years later, following the kind outreach from my friend, we have since mended fences, and our daughters even became pen pals. Now THAT is funny to me.

God was there, setting the stage during Angie's similar heartbreak. God had to disrupt her current path to lay the steps for her future, in His time. Somewhere in that process, Angie ended up being, essentially, another roommate and a dear friend to me. Spring break was fast approaching, and I was headed to Florida to meet my family and then drive to Atlanta, GA, for a NASCAR race. Angie loved NASCAR and asked if she could come too. We thought, "Why not?" So, she came along for the ride. Little did we know that it would change her life forever.

While we were there, she met my sister Stephanie's husband's brother, Mark. I think Mark was smitten from the beginning, but Angie was resistant. When Mark asked Matt to ask Steph to ask me to ask Angie for her phone number, she was clear.

*"He can call me, but I don't 'like him,' like him."*

They've been married for over ten years now and have beautiful twin girls.

Literally, if God hadn't had Jean and Nikki place that advertisement and then called me to answer it, this world would have seven fewer beautiful children. Heartbreak is worth it, and frankly, I welcome it if it leads me, or the people I care about, to follow God's plan for a life they could never have dreamed up for themselves.

# NASHVILLE, TN 2006

*My Nashville Anniversary*

June 2nd, 2006, is my "Nashville Anniversary." I think most people who move to Nashville in hopes of realizing their dreams also keep track of and celebrate the day it became their home. Nashville is the only city I remember the precise date that I moved to it. People often ask me, "What's your best advice to someone who wants to make it in the music industry?" My answer is straightforward, and it always stays the same. "Move here. You can't go swimming if you're not in the water." That's what I did, and it's the first conscious decision that set me up for success. In my senior year of college, I had to fulfill an internship requirement for my music business degree. I was intentionally saving it for my last semester so that if I were offered a job in Nashville, I'd be able to accept it and stay there. One of the best parts of my education, really THE best part of my education, was the ability to be a part of MEISA, the student component of the Music Entertainment Industry Educators Association (Belmont University). Being a member of MEISA allowed me to attend conferences across the country. The most impactful event for me occurred in Miami, Florida, at the University of Miami. I was attending a panel on A&R, and one of the panelists was the president of a new record label in Nashville called Equity Music Group. As I listened to Mike Kraski talking about the partnership with country music star Clint Black and the way they worked and supported their acts, including Little Big Town, Mark Wills, and Carolyn Dawn Johnson, I knew this was the company I wanted to begin my career with, so I asked him if I could. Mike kindly gave me his card and instructions on how to set up an interview in Nashville to intern for the label.

In April of 2005, my sister Steph met me in Nashville to help me find an apartment and to be my support system while I sought after my internship. I didn't know if I'd land the one I was hoping for, so I made 30 packets and was prepared to go door to door to try and secure one. Thankfully, I was offered the internship during the interview and couldn't have been happier. With my sister's help, we nailed down my first apartment, and I went back to North Dakota a day early because we accomplished everything so quickly. In less than two months after that trip, just as the CMA Music Festival kicked off, I became a Nashville resident.

*My Planet*

When it was time to leave my home in North Dakota, I celebrated a fun final weekend there with friends and then said goodbye. My parents helped me pack up my navy-blue Hyundai Sonata, and they loaded up another vehicle. Together with my little niece Jaida, we made the 21-hour trek to Nashville. The thing I remember most about that time is the feeling of excitement. When I saw the green sign on the interstate that said, "Nashville 17." I remember being overwhelmed, not by sadness or fear but by the feeling of coming home. I felt like I was landing on my planet. A place where all the "weird music people" or "creative types" from across the country, and a few Nashville natives, live as "the normal people." I didn't know how right I was, but He did.

Early on in my adventure, I made many friends through my internship and within the music industry. Some of my fondest memories of that time included The Stage on Broadway. Nashville's Broadway is a place like no other, populated with aspiring songwriters and artists playing for tips in the Honky Tonks to an audience filled with tourists, convention attendees, and very possibly country music stars. A LOT is going on all the time, and it can be effortless to get caught up in all the excitement.

Back then, in the early 2000s, we used to go to The Stage every Monday night for what we called "Rock Night." Monday nights are like Friday nights for people in the industry who are on the road because they work all weekend. One Monday night in particular, I was experiencing homesickness and missing people from North Dakota, so I decided to catch up with a friend from home for spiritual encouragement.

Josh and I went to high school together, and although I didn't see it then, I get it now. Josh and his brother are priests, and he is someone whose story and insight encourage me. As we were texting about my move to Nashville, Father Waltz said something that still stays in my head.

He said, "It's great that you moved to Nashville to bring light to a place of darkness."

I thought, "Um, no, I didn't. I moved to Nashville to get a great job in the music industry and live my dream life filled with country music stars."

Josh may not be a prophet, but he certainly had more faith in God's plan for me than I did. How do I know? Well, here I sit writing this chapter, not in First Class but in Delta Comfort, on my way to New York City for work. Our country star is performing on Good Morning America's Summer Concert Series tomorrow, and I'm writing my testimony about how great God is if only you can let go and let His will be done.

*He Knew*

I've said before that I'm so thankful that God is God, and I am not. He's the driving force in my life, and I'm like the speed bumps and obstacles that He navigates around. Nevertheless, He prevails and provides even when we don't know that's what he's doing.

During my first ten years in Music City, I lived in several parts of Nashville, one of which was an area that I loved called Nippers Corner. I lived there with a friend who purchased a townhouse and let me move in since we were hanging out so much anyway. I lived quite a way out of the city. (In real life, I was 15 minutes from downtown, so that's nothing to complain about.)

Although we had a blast living together, things change over time, and people change, too. I knew it was time for me to venture out on my own, so when an apartment became available in the trendy part of Nashville called "The Gulch." I knew I had to take it, and in 2007 I did. I quickly discovered that the building was unique, and looking back on it, I realize now it was an anointed decision. Four years before it became my biggest, smallest asset, coming in just under 700 square feet, God laid a solid foundation for me.

Things were looking good. After finishing my internship, I officially began my career in the music industry. After bouncing around a few places – an independent PR firm, a record label that went under, a Christian record label, and a temp agency – I landed at my new professional home as an assistant to a woman who owned and operated an independent boutique publicity and marketing firm. I spent almost four years there, meeting new people and building relationships that mean the world to me today. I experienced love, laughter, tears, accomplishments, disappointments, and both the highest highs and the lowest lows in my life up to that point.

It's funny how people pop in and out of lives, and it so often makes me wonder, "Why now?" Jesse is one of those people for me. He was living in California at the time and came to Nashville a few times for work to network and generate leads for his business. I remember the first time Jesse reached out to me. I was so excited to see him because he was a piece of home for me. We're both from North Dakota and went to high school together. We knew so many of the same people, some being my dearest friends, and I believed we'd have a blast catching up.

When he arrived in town, I came down with strep throat and had to cancel. It disappointed me so much that I made sure to be available the next time, and I was right. We did have an incredible time together. After that, we continued talking and would make time for each other when we were in the same city.

I remember being happy after texting him one day, and the question returned. "Why? Why did God bring Jesse back into my life?" Then I thought, "Wouldn't it be weird if God brought him back into my life to help me get through losing my dad?" There is a 17-year age gap between my parents. Throughout my entire life, I always assumed that my Dad would pass away before my mom. Everyone who knows me knows that math is not my jam, but a 17-year age gap was a pretty safe bet that I was right. I let the thought go and pulled out of the Wendy's drive-through on West End.

The following day was Sunday, and it was also the week of Thanksgiving. For whatever reason, I didn't do anything for Thanksgiving that year aside from ordering pizza and eating whipped cream from a can with cranberry sauce. Actually, I know why. I was legit poor. There were weeks when I 100% had to call home and ask someone to send me grocery money or order me a pizza. It is not easy to live on $22,500 a year, and I was struggling but advancing in my role at work and "Living the dream."

My phone rang, "Mom & Dad" showed up on my cell phone's caller ID, so I picked up. Although this conversation made no sense to me, I remember every word.

"Hello," I said.

"Dawn, it's Dad," said my father, Sam.

"Yeah, I figured that when my phone said, 'Mom and Dad,' and then you said, 'Dawn.' I replied with my lovely sarcastic tone, well in place for a Sunday morning.

He said, "Dawn, I have some bad news."

Immediately, I knew that someone in my family had passed away, and my mind raced toward the familiar faces of older relatives. I think about my Grandma T, my great Uncle Bob, my Aunt Arlys…as my wondering mind was interrupted by my dad saying,

"Your mom died."

"Who?" I said.

"Your Mom."

"Who?" I asked again. It was as if he had said a word I had never heard before or a word that made no logical sense whatsoever, like, "Your paper clip died."

"Your mother." He said.

With the release of those words from his breath, my heart fell to the concrete floor and my knees along with it, and I wailed, bursting into tears in my bedroom.

My Dad doesn't do great with us girls if we turn into emotional messes of his daughters, and so I knew I had to pull myself together long enough to listen to what I could do to help him at that moment. He needed a few phone numbers from me, and he needed my sister Kristy and me to call Steph.

Our call to Steph was another conversation I distinctly remember because it was very similar to the one I just had.

Steph was at work when Kristy and I called her on a three-way call. She, too, didn't understand, and to this day, it's hard to accept as reality.

My next call was to my boss. I don't even know why I called her first, other than that my life was utterly revolving around work. I called her crying and couldn't say the words clearly. When I eventually uttered them, she hung up the phone and came right over.

While she helped me process this devastating information, we were interrupted by a phone call I had to take. As I was talking, she began looking for plane tickets and got me on a flight out of Nashville that evening on a bereavement fare. I didn't ask her to; I didn't even know it was an option. I wasn't thinking clearly enough to realize I needed to leave. I thanked her for the gift and immediately went home to North Dakota. I was a puddle on the two flights required to get me from Nashville to Bismarck, connecting in Minneapolis, MN. I remember I was sitting very close to the front of the plane, crying and drinking Bloody Marys. It was a sad and lonely flight, although the people around me tried to make me feel better. Now, I try diligently not to fly on November 29th and to do something good for myself instead.

When I walked in the front door and stood in the home I grew up in, it was surreal. I can't explain how terribly sad it is to walk into your home, in the same rooms that someone you love stood in hours before, only to know that they will never be there again. I could feel it in the air. Mom had succumbed to a pulmonary embolism and passed away peacefully.

That night, as I lay down to go to sleep with a damp face from tear-filled eyes and a heavy heart, I did it with a lifeline.

My cell phone chimed with an alert for a text message. I'd open Jesse's messages from California, and something always made me smile: a photo of a semi-truck with my name on the side, a funny joke, or a silly picture.

It wasn't a "what if." God put Jesse in my life at that time to help me get through losing my mom, and that's precisely what he helped me do.

# TURN THE PAGE, 2010

*Going Home*

After what felt like forever being back in North Dakota, in reality, it was only about a month; it was time for me to go home. My sister Kristy and I stayed to help our family the best we could, and we knew backup was coming soon. My sister Stephanie and her husband Matt decided to uproot their lives in Florida to move back to North Dakota to help take care of our father and nieces Jaida and Kezawin, whom my parents were raising when my mom suddenly passed. It was a freezing January in North Dakota when the Sullivan's packed up their 2-year-old daughter Sami and moved their whole world back to Bismarck.

One benefit of being close to someone from your hometown is the holidays. While I was home in North Dakota going through the loss of my mom, Jesse was also coming back for the holidays. Usually, around Christmas, many of us from high school get together and go out at least one night and have an epic time. That year was no exception, and it was fun having Jesse there with us and being supportive in person.

*LA Sunshine*

Once I was back in Nashville, Jesse had plans to come to town for work, and I couldn't have been happier to have him around. Coming back here with my heart still in North Dakota was weird, but I received so much support from friends in Nashville and others who reached out via Facebook, including some I met in second grade. This digital world is wild when it comes to that.

*It Just Got Real*

After he left town, it got real for me. My ray of sunshine disappeared, out of sight anyway, and the dark clouds rolled in. Nights were the worst. I'd lay in bed just wondering why that happened and trying to comprehend that my mom was gone. Realizing that I'd never in this life get a hug from her again. That reality would, and still sometimes does, simultaneously cause me to lose my breath under a crushing weight in my chest and a parade of tears. Those nights were long and sad. Every day, I went to a job that sometimes made me smile, but overall, I was miserable at. I worked a lot, was still poor, and was missing my ray of sunshine being around in person. Around this time, someone I had known a few years ago began contacting me to get together. Since I was preoccupied with everything else and talked to Jesse regularly, I didn't take him up on his offer.

Shortly after that, I was not doing well. I was drinking too much and making terrible choices, and I was utterly lost. To be totally honest, I don't remember calling on God much or trusting in Him that this was happening as a part of His will and His plan for my life. I just felt so alone. All those feelings affected my conversations on the West Coast, and ultimately, yet amicably, it was time to let go of him, too. I've always said that I cared so much for Jesse that I felt like we were in a plane, flying okay but losing elevation. I knew we'd crash hard if I continued with him, and I didn't want that for us. So that was that. One Sunday morning, it was all over.

32

*Will You Share Your Story?*

I was on set for a photoshoot with one of my artists when I began visiting with the editor of a magazine called *Her Nashville*. She asked me what was going on with me these days. I told her everything that was happening, including the loss of my mother. For some reason, my story struck a chord with her, and she asked me if I'd write it for the magazine, offering my perspective as I approached my first Mother's Day without my mom. I was honored and humbled by the request but thought I was not qualified to do that. I discussed it with my sisters and decided that if we could write it as a collective from each of us, I'd give it a shot. They agreed, and we wrote "A Mother's Legacy" for *Her Nashville*.

As our first Mother's Day approached, we had a light at the end of the tunnel. Stephanie, Kristy, and I were going to Hawaii for our friend's wedding. It was an overdue vacation for all of us, and we were looking forward to it. We spent several days on the big island, and while we were there, we celebrated Mom. Our mother LOVED the ocean and collected lighthouses. Whenever we were near the ocean, we'd think of her and call so she could hear the waves. On that trip, Stephanie brought us some ashes we could scatter or keep with us as we continued without her. While we were in Hawaii that April, the *Her Nashville* piece came out online, and we read it together, which was special.

*A Mother's Day Surprise*

After Hawaii, I came home and went to one of my best girlfriends' houses to ease back into real life and not be alone after my trip. While there, I got a message from "Ben," the guy I mentioned earlier. He asked what I was doing, and I told him I was grilling out at a friend's house.

Then he said, "Go home. I'm coming over."

That's what I did. I left my friend's house, went home to my loft apartment in Nashville, and waited to see someone I hadn't seen in about two years.

He didn't get to my apartment until near or after midnight. I remember thinking how good-looking he was, and I was pleased to see him again. We visited for a while, and then things escalated quickly. I remember so many of my decisions from that night. Only a couple of days later, I knew things were different, and the feeling in my heart was almost immediate. I knew we had conceived a child, and it happened to occur on Mother's Day, the very first one without my mom.

If I'm being honest, I think I said "yes" that night for several reasons. My heart was sad. I missed my mom, was still trying to get over not having Jesse in my life, and was approaching 30. I wanted the right guy (who I still know is out there for me), but I didn't know where he was. If I'm being honest, at that moment, I just wanted to feel, to be wanted, and to be held.

*OMG*

I felt so early on that I was pregnant that I even told "Ben" before taking my first test. A day or two later, I drove to CVS and bought a test. Somehow, I messed it up, and the results were not clear. So, I returned to CVS, got another test, and drove home to retake it.

"Darn, somehow I didn't get a good enough sample on the stick," so it was blank. Then, I just tried to re-do the same test, and the results were inconclusive again. So, back to CVS, this time, I bought a 5-pack. As I waited 3 minutes for my 3rd test to process, I read something in the directions that made the hairs on my arm stand up, and my heart skipped a beat. "Pregnant: Two Pink Lines appear in the Easy Read Result Window. Note: One line may be lighter than the other."

I thought, "Um, so, does that mean I just took two POSITIVE pregnancy tests and didn't know how to interpret the results?"

My timer went off, and I walked toward the bathroom, praying. "Dear Heavenly Father, please be with me as I walk through these doors and read the results of this test. I am so scared nevertheless, let Thy will be done." This time, I got the pregnancy test for dummies, and it said, "Pregnant."

*Fear and Anger*

There it was. OMG. Pregnant. The next thing I remember is standing outside on my balcony, going from one concerned ear to another as I confided in two of my sisters and a handful of trusted friends. I knew they all loved me and wanted what was best for me, but I think they were all scared for me, too. I had taken a lot of risks to get to where I was, poor lifestyle choices aside, and I was chasing my dream in the music industry in Nashville. Now, that could all go away. What if I had to quit and move home to North Dakota?

I'm not proud of this, but I did call Planned Parenthood a knee-jerk reaction, and I made an appointment for the following week.

*The Questions*

The next day, I was lying on my couch and experienced one of the few times in my life that I believe God spoke right into my heart. It went a lot like this.

God: Dawn, what if you are having twins? Could you abort two babies?"

Me: "No!"

God: "What's the difference between one and two?"

Me: "Nothing."

So, I started researching adoption at that very moment. During this conversation with God, "Ben" was texting me, wanting to know more about my plans, still trying to convince me to have an abortion. He said he would help pay for it and wanted to go with me when I had it done. I told him that I was considering adoption instead, and "Ben" was furious. Although he was at work, he said, "I'm coming over. We need to talk about this."

Before he arrived at my door, God had another message for me.

God: "Dawn, when your baby is six months old, you will be 30. How many 30-year-olds are just giving away their children? You're not a teenager!"

"Ben" knocked on my door, still wearing his work clothes, bless his heart, and looking scared. He first hugged me and said it was nice to see me, then came inside. He desperately pleaded with me not to have this baby. I told him,

*"I wouldn't choose to be pregnant right now, but I can't choose not to be."*

When I asked him why he was so against it if I was considering adoption, he said, "Because I don't want to have a child in this world that I'm not a father to." All I could think to say to him was, "That's your choice, and this was mine." He went on to promise me that he'd be there for me every step of the way. He'd help pay. He'd come to the appointment. He'd stay with me every night until I felt better. That one made me laugh. I immediately imagined him ditching me in the parking lot minutes after they had called my name for the procedure, with dirt flying up from his car's wheels as he peeled out.

When he left, his last words were, "Dawn, please don't do this. Please don't have this baby. Promise me you'll think about it."

After "Ben" left me in my apartment, I picked up my conversation with God, already knowing the answer.

I honestly don't know why I asked Him so  many questions. I always knew I wanted to be a mom, and if I ever faced that decision, I'd only have one option.

I didn't know what would happen the second I said, "Okay, I'm going to have a baby" out loud. The moment I uttered those words, a peace I can't explain covered me like a blanket.

*Saying Yes*

I lived 2,000 miles from home, barely making ends meet, chasing my dream in Nashville, TN. Although I was where I wanted to be, it was hard, and I often didn't have enough money to buy groceries. Sitting on my bed, alone, scared, and essentially poor, I accepted God's plan for my life. I was in a terrible situation without maternity insurance or a real plan; all I knew was the peace from God and that everything would be okay.

Imagine what I could be like if I let God do a little work. *"It's not about how rusty the wreck is but how good the artist is."* – Mike Glenn, Senior Pastor at Brentwood Baptist Church

That night, and every night of my pregnancy, I slept with a pillow between me and the edge of the bed. I didn't want to fall off and hurt the baby. I was going to be a mother, and I was already falling in love.

I can't leave this moment without telling you something that is the essence of my testimony.

When I was on that balcony, crying, terrified that I was a failure and sure that I had let people down, I had it all wrong. In the same breath that I thought my dreams were being ripped away from me, God was handing me more than I could have ever even known to dream. All I had to do was say "Yes" to trusting His plan.

If I had followed through with my plans and let fear take the wheel, *I* would have been the person who destroyed my life.

# A New Book 2010



*The Stairs of a Baptist Church*

As someone raised in the Catholic church, the Baptist church has been in my life at crucial moments. I officially "Invited Jesus into my heart at a Baptist Bible camp," and I physically felt that happen. (I've tried to recreate that sensation, but it hasn't worked.) On this day in the summer of 2010, it was less of a heartwarming experience. I decided to have a baby and was 100% at peace with it. I wasn't far along in my pregnancy, but I told my boss about it anyway. I had worked for her company for over three years and was her most senior employee. She told me once, "As long as I have a company, you have a job." I enjoyed most of what I did at her company in PR and Marketing, but I wasn't making nearly enough money to support a family. I'd need a huge raise or permission to leave and get a new job to make ends meet when the time came.

Our usual thing for "private meetings" was to take it outside and go for a walk. That sunny Friday, we were headed down the street, and I slowly started framing what I planned to say to her. We sat on the stairs of an old building nearby, and I said to my boss, "I am going to have a baby." She was shocked. With her being a mother of two kids herself, I didn't know what to expect going into the conversation, but it certainly wasn't what followed. She responded to me by telling me to stop telling people that I was having a baby. She then said that it's not a baby anyway; it's just a divided cell. I'll never forget these words: "Having a baby will close doors for you personally and professionally." Then we walked back to the office. Years later, I drove by that old building again and realized where the conversation had happened: on the back stairs of a Baptist church.

### *A Photo Is Worth a Thousand Words*

The day I booked a photoshoot with my friend and photographer Bev Moser to help me get an updated headshot and document the final days of not looking pregnant, neither of us knew how impactful it would turn out to be. Bev was a single mom to a little boy and was successful in Nashville. I was curious about how that worked for her, so, between trying to get shots where I was making normal faces, I peppered her with questions in sunny Centennial Park. It wasn't until months later that I shared with her that I was about to become a mom.

*"I knew it!"* she beamed. *"I just had a feeling when you were so interested in our story and had so many questions."*

After Ev was born, we went back to Centennial Park with Bev several times for photos together, including the image on the cover of this book.

### *The Calls*

Once I decided it was time to go public with my pregnancy, I needed to make two calls. The first to my Dad and then my mom's mom, Grandma T.

My Dad was in his late 70s, and I'd started to feel protective of him and his health as he aged. I was more careful to tell him to watch his step or to "look out," which I would never have done when we were both younger. Along those same lines, I didn't want him to have a heart attack when I told him he was about to become a grandpa again for the 16th time. To ease the shock, I wanted him to be in a comfortable place with no other distractions, where he was sitting down to hear my news.

The day I called him, I was very nervous. Stephanie answered the phone and told me Dad was waiting to hear from me in his room. She took the phone to my Dad, and I was so scared while I waited for him to come on the line.

"Hi, honey," Dad said. "So, why did your sister send me to my room with a bowl of ice cream?"

I thought the ice cream was a nice touch on her part.

"Dad, I have to tell you something, and I'm scared." I started to cry.

"What's wrong?" he said.

I answered, "Well, Dad, I'm going to have a baby."

"You are?" He exclaimed, "Congratulations!"

"Thank you!" I said with a laugh while crying.

We continued talking for a few more minutes before he told me he loved me and that I'd be a great mom. I couldn't have asked for that conversation to go any better, and I was so relieved to have it with him.

Next was Grandma. I called her up and said the same thing to her. She replied much the same as my Dad, but I could hear more concern in her voice. One thing that differed in the conversation with my grandma was that she told me something else.

"Thank you," Grandma said.

"For what?" I asked her.

"For deciding to have the baby and not the alternative."

It meant so much to me to hear that from my grandma because I looked up to her so much, and she's been such an excellent example for me as a Christian woman. I was anxious about disappointing her and my father, instead their support meant the world to me.

With those two calls done, I was at peace and not worried about disappointing my family. I made a couple more FYI calls to people I felt should hear the news from me rather than finding out on Facebook or from someone else, and things felt good.

One person who continued to oppose my choice, however, was "Ben." He was straight-up mad at me when I told him that I was keeping the baby. He sent me text messages swearing at me, or he'd call and say to me that I was a b!t$h and that I was ruining his life. I knew he was mad, but I thought, given time, surely, he'd come around and chill out before the baby was born. In the meantime, I looked over my shoulder a lot, especially in my parking lot when I'd get home late after work.

June brought two of my favorite events in Nashville, the CMA Music Festival and the All About Music Film and TV Retreat. When my mom was still living, she and my Dad would come down for the CMA Music Festival, and it was an extraordinary time for me looking back. Although I wasn't working directly with the artists at the festival then, I was on my way, and my mom could see some of her favorite artists perform. Every year, when it rolls around, I think of her and how proud she'd be of me for where I am now.

In June of 2011, however, I was in a different place. I was knocked up and beginning to tell my friends in the music industry. All About Music was one of my absolute favorite industry events. It's once a year in Nashville when my dear friend Emmit Martin would bring in the film/tv industry's top music supervisors for three days of music, networking, and unimaginable fun. At this year's event, I was not drinking due to my pregnancy but enjoyed it just as much. The day after the retreat, I met one of my friends from LA for breakfast. I told Andrea Von Forester how this year was a little different for me because I wasn't drinking.

"I don't drink." She said.

"What?" I replied. "You don't drink?" I had never noticed because she was always having fun with the rest of us at the same events. Then I told her why I wasn't drinking.

"I'm going to have a baby," I said.

Andrea smiled. "The Last time we talked, you said you couldn't get a dog because you didn't have time, and now, you're going to have a baby!"

I laughed. I forgot I had said that to her, but I did.

Marianne Goode was another of my friends from LA who significantly impacted me during my early pregnancy. She was the VP of Music at Lifetime Television and someone I look up to as a woman in this industry. Honestly, I wasn't sure how she'd respond to me. Would it be a similar reaction to my boss'?

I remember Marianne's very kind face lighting up with a smile and telling me how happy she was for me. Then she grew more serious and said, "You can do this, and you will be an incredible mother. Do you hear me?"

I teared up and said, "Yes, thank you."

The fact that she had so much confidence in me was inspiring and boosted mine.

I am forever thankful to Emmit for bringing so many incredible people into my world, who have remained with me all these years. Himself included. I never could have known how big a role we would play in each other's lives when I first reached out to him for an artist slot at his event.

Once my boss knew that I was 100% having and keeping my baby, we had another talk over breakfast at Union Station Hotel. It was a light discussion about money, which is always fun. I explained to her that I'd need to make significantly more money or her blessing to look for a new job. She gave me that blessing, and I casually began looking in the late summer of 2010.

*Resources in Tennessee*

So, what do you do when you have no money and you're going to have a baby? You Google. After doing a fair share of internet research, I came upon CoverKids, a government insurance program in Tennessee that allowed me to have the doctor of my choice with excellent medical care throughout my pregnancy. CoverKids offers free health coverage for pregnant women and children who do not have insurance and who do not qualify for TennCare. This coverage was my first sign and actual proof that this could be okay!

I encourage every woman who finds herself in the position I was in to look into this Tennessee program or for something similar to this in the other 49.

Additionally, the Hope Clinic for Women is another resource I highly encourage women to reach out to for counsel and a friendly, understanding, and calm voice on the other end of the line.

Deciding to bring a child into the world, or not, is a forever decision. Take a moment to explore the possibilities.

*The Phone Call*

The few times I've needed a new opportunity in the music industry, I've searched for one in the same simple way. I write an email to all of my contacts, letting them know I'm looking and asking for their input and insight on possible places where I could interview. On Sunday night in September 2010, I did just that.

*"Good evening,*

*I hope this finds you all well and enjoying your Sunday. It was a great day for the Titans!*

*I've been working with {company} for almost four years now, and I'm writing today because it's time for me to take on another exciting challenge in my career, and I'm hoping that you may know of an opportunity for me. My experience is heavy in PR, marketing, social media, film, and television licensing, and I have additional on-the-road experience providing PR and merchandise services.*

*I'm attaching my resume, and I would truly appreciate any leads you may be able to send my way.*

*Thank you in advance for your time, friendship, and support.*

*Have a wonderful week!*

*Warm regards,*
*Dawn"*

The following day, I was at work when I received a call from my boss.

"What did you do?" She asked.

"What are you talking about?" I answered.

She continued, "Why are people calling me and asking if I'm closing my company?"

I had no idea what to say, and after a moment, I told her about the email I sent the night before. I reminded her that we talked about this: either I'd need to make significantly more money, or I needed her permission to seek another opportunity, to which she agreed. She wasn't happy with my answer and told me I should have let her read my email.

"Well, have you found one?" she asked irritated.

"No," I replied.

I was about six months pregnant, which she reminded me of when she retorted with this epic condemnation. "No one is going to hire you this late in pregnancy; you do know that. Right?"

Shocked and a little pissed off, I quickly responded, "No. I don't know that."

We ended the phone call, and she didn't bring up my pregnancy again unless someone else said something about it first.

*Status Update*

Nowadays, it takes a push of a button to send ripples into the world, or at least our personal lives. After one of the most incredible doctor visits I've ever had, I learned I was to become a mama to a precious little girl and couldn't keep the news to myself any longer. So naturally, I took it to Facebook with a post on September 16th, 2010. God gave me a gift, and it felt so good to proudly and peacefully let people in on it. Looking back, I had no idea of the impact this little ladybug would have on my future social media posts.

New Year's Eve had come and gone, and it was January of 2011. I had worked at this company for almost four years, and it looked like I would hit that mile marker. Although I had a longshot "dream lead" in play, I didn't have a job lined up, and I was running out of time. I still felt total peace about my decision and let each day pass without worrying too much. It was time to consider my maternity leave and what salary I would need to make ends meet. I knew I would not quit without having a job lined up, so I fully intended to have the baby and return to my current position.

Two weeks before my due date, God stepped in and changed my life.

My boss asked me if we could meet for breakfast that Friday to discuss my leave and salary in the new year. Of course, I agreed and planned on it for the next morning. Then we bumped it to lunch and, ultimately, dinner.

We had a nice dinner and ate EVERYTHING: appetizers, main course, dessert, and coffee. Towards the end of the meal, I joked about our evening, saying we ate so much that it was like a "Last Meal," only to find out that was a telling Freudian slip.

"That's an interesting segue," she chimed in, "because you know I'm not going to be able to meet your salary requirement."

"Huh?" I thought to myself. "Did she just fire me?"

She continued talking, and I tuned in just in time to hear her say something about a severance package.

"She just fired me," I told myself.

My due date was two weeks away. This moment is where total panic, tears, labored breathing (possibly early labor itself), and the feeling of absolute desertion should have hit me hard.

But it didn't.

It was almost like the light and peace of God broke through the restaurant's ceiling and completely covered me, wrapping me up like a blanket. All I heard from her was that I was getting out, a light was at the end of the tunnel, and the next book of my life was about to begin.

I didn't even mind that she wrapped up the conversation by telling me to plan on coming in for the next two weeks to train the new guy.

Although I did feel peace with this, I also felt very betrayed by my boss. I thought we had a strong personal and professional relationship that she just threw away. That was how I felt on the personal side. On the business side, I knew we were playing a game of chicken: either I would get a new job and leave, or she would lay me off.

*First Day of Fired*

My "first day of fired" was pretty uneventful. I was happy and mentally preparing for the life path that I was faithfully walking. Each day that passed was closer to the Thursday before my due date. That Thursday had extreme significance because it was the day my sister Stephanie arrived in Nashville to be with me for the delivery of the baby.

I say the baby because I hadn't committed to her name, although Evelyn was starting to take hold in the final days. I told her every night, "Now listen to me, little lady; you need to wait until Auntie Stephy gets here before you come out!" It meant the world to me to know that she would be here to step into the role that my mother would have had if she was still alive, as my mom did when Steph had her first child. Looking back, I don't even think I asked her to come. She just told me and asked me about dates, and I remember thinking, "What? You're going to fly here to be with me?" It was second nature to her, and I should have known because that's the same attitude, strength, and faith that Steph had when she told my sisters and me that she was moving home from Florida with her husband and young daughter to step into the role as caregiver and that my mom was carrying before she passed. They moved back to add a little 8-year-old girl, my niece Jaida, to their family and help be there for our 74-year-old father.

### Final Day of Fired – 1/28/11

The baby took directions well and stayed put until her auntie arrived on Thursday. We had a lot of plans before my due date the following Monday, but we started with the all-important dinner at Chili's so Steph could have the chips and salsa. God was working here, too, because it was on this trip that I spent a brief amount of time pregnant; at the same time, my sister was also pregnant. She was three months along, which meant my daughter would be six months older than her new cousin. The next day was my "final day of fired," a seemingly normal Friday, except I finally had a job interview! My interview was at 9 am, and I had a noon doctor's appointment, followed by going into the office to finally leave officially.

The interview was with the "dream lead" company I so badly wanted to work for, and I had an interview with the new CEO, Gordon Kerr.

Trying to make an excellent first impression, I brought doughnuts, a decision that had an enormous, unintended consequence.

When I walked into the building at 12 Music Circle South in the heart of Music Row, I realized I had been there several years before for Category Five Records' studio reopening. All of a sudden, I felt a little overwhelmed, but I took my seat at the table for my interview and gave my anxiety up to God.

The interview was typical as far as interviews go, but I remember immediately feeling connected with the CEO and thinking how kind and wise he appeared to be. Then it all went askew, and my cool went right out the window with one question.

"Who is your hero?" he asked me.

"My hero?" I repeated, and suddenly, my head and heart were flooded with thoughts and images of my mom.

"My mom," I answered just before beginning to cry.

"I'm sorry," I squeaked out before uttering the words not usually recommended in a job interview. "My mom recently passed away, and I'm going to have a baby."

"Don't have one now!" he joked while handing me a box of tissues. While wiping my eyes and laughing to cover some embarrassment, I answered him, "Do you like this chair?" joking that I may have the baby right there.

As we were getting back on track, the CEO told me that he didn't ask me a fair question for a job interview, and that's the point. This question elicits an emotional response, and if it doesn't, and the recipient doesn't have a hero to name, then he doesn't want that person working for him. We all need someone to look up to, and it was in that seemingly failed interview that I realized I wanted to be a part of his team.

Driving away from the interview, the two minutes it took me to get home to pick up my sister and head to my doctor's appointment, I reflected on how I thought it went. I remember going around the roundabout at Música and thinking, "Well, I probably don't deserve to be there, but I'm happy with how that went." Whether or not I landed the job, I knew I did my best, and the rest was in God's hands. I again was entirely covered in an almost naïve peace.

I pulled into my apartment's parking lot and walked towards the industrial front door to go inside and meet my sister. It was almost time for my doctor's appointment. Walking through the parking lot, I remember feeling a lot of pressure from the baby and thinking, "She has to be ready to come out soon. I can almost feel her in my toes!"

We arrived at my doctor's office and met with Dr. Erin Yu. She came to be my doctor on the recommendation of Mandy, one of my best friends in Nashville and she was another Godsend. I had an OBGYN before Dr. Yu, but when I found out I was pregnant and had an unfulfilled birth control prescription in my purse, I could imagine how that conversation would go if I returned to him.

"Oh! Do you mean this piece of paper isn't a magic protective shield? I need to fill it and take it?"

As Stephanie and I sat waiting for my doctor to come in, I remember being excited for them to meet. I am so thankful that God allowed Stephanie to be with me at that point because I was about to be doubly blindsided.

Dr. Yu came into the room, and we exchanged pleasantries. Then, it got real.

"Well, Dawn," she said. "You're experiencing excessive swelling in your feet, and you have traces of protein in your urine, which means preeclampsia is setting in. So, we need to think about having this baby."

Now, clearly, I'm not a doctor, and my sister hadn't started nursing school yet, so I wasn't entirely aware of what any of that meant, which was apparent when I answered her.

"Well, my sister is here now, and my due date is Monday; I'm good whenever."

Dr. Yu smiled and said," No, you need to go to the hospital, and we're going to induce you now."

"You mean I don't have to go to my 'final day of fired!?'" I asked.

"No, she said, you can run home and grab some things, but then you'll need to come back and register in the hospital."

*The Delivery*

All of a sudden, it was getting exciting. Then came the second surprise.

"There's one more thing," she said. "I am supposed to be leaving today for a family vacation with my husband and the boys…"

I knew this was an important trip for her and her family, so I thanked her when she said she'd stay as long as possible and see how I was progressing.

After a speedy trip home, I grabbed a few things and quickly shaved my legs. Ha-ha, that's a true story. Then we were off to check into Baptist Hospital. It was time for us to meet this baby! Yet, it was weird because I felt like I was checking into a hotel. There was no rush of my water breaking, no contractions, just signing some papers and going to our room.

My sister Jacky met us at the hospital, and she and Stephanie kept me in good spirits as we waited and waited for things to progress. The delivery was long, and the amount of time her delivery was taking, coupled with the complications that led to my being induced, things got a little scary towards the end.

Most people know that when you deliver a baby, you push in three sets of 10. I owned the 1st two sets, but by the time I came around to set 3, I felt like I was making all the noise and making a funny face, and that was about it. I was so tired. Finally, my doctor had me stop.

I looked at my sister Stephanie as I started to feel bad that I couldn't do what I was supposed to, and I was beginning to feel scared that I would need a C-section. I asked my sister, "Isn't there a class or something to help with pushing?" "Yes," she said. "It's called Lamaze, and you didn't take it!" And we both laughed.

I was out of energy from pushing, my fever was beginning to spike, and Ev was not coming out like she was supposed to and was in distress. Finally, the doctor made the call to do an episiotomy and used the forceps to complete the delivery.

After that, it was a mere moment, at 3:48 am, that Evelyn entered the world. She was 6lbs 11oz and 20 inches long. I'd had several dreams about her but had no idea what she'd look like. Her beauty took me aback. She did suffer a broken clavicle from the delivery and came out blowing bubbles, but other than that, she was perfect. Then, she was rushed away to the NIC Unit for monitoring while I was tended to.

It was hours before I saw her again, this time in my hospital room. Yes, I needed time to rest and recover from the delivery, but I also wanted her back in my sight. If I had to describe the feeling of not having her near me, my best attempt was to say it felt like I was missing a part of me. "Oh, where is my leg? I need my leg!" It was that huge of a void.

Once she was with me again, I began to feel better. I remember showering and thinking, "Well, I wouldn't want to do this every weekend, but I'd do it again!"

# Chapter 1, 2011

*We're Home*

Stephanie stayed with me for about a week and a half after Evie was born, and I was thankful. Although, at times, I may not have acted like it. Those first couple of weeks were exhausting, and I would get crabby at times from lack of sleep and frustration in the first few days from not being able to nurse my tiny baby. It was intensely pulling on my heart to nurse her, giving her the best possible start in life, so it was maddening when we had to give her a little formula because I couldn't do it. I was angry and sad.

That night, after Evie and Steph were asleep, I sat up on the couch trying to pump, and I sobbed. It was then that I just let go and prayed, begging for the Lord to get me through this moment and to make my body do what it was supposed to so I could feed my baby. Exhausted, I soon fell asleep as well. The next morning was a new day; the milk came in, and I never had a problem with nursing again.

*Supermarket Sweep*

In the first week of being home after having the baby, I did two things I would recommend to anyone in a similar place: jobless and with another little mouth to feed. I filed for unemployment and registered with WIC. The Special Supplemental Nutrition Program for Women, Infants, and Children (WIC) provides Federal grants to States for supplemental foods, health care referrals, and nutrition education for low-income pregnant, breastfeeding, and non-breastfeeding postpartum women and to infants and children up to age five who are found to be at nutritional risk.

Because of those two steps, I received unemployment checks to help cover costs. Every month, I received certain items like milk, eggs, etc., and I had an allotment for other food items. Now, this was one of my favorite parts. My monthly food budget allotment from WIC was more than I was used to spending for food, so I bought what I needed, and then I went into "Supermarket Sweep" mode and filled up my cart with baby food and snack items for every stage of the first year. In the first few months after Evelyn was born, I purchased baby food veggies & fruit, cereal, snacks, and other pantry items, ultimately taking the burden off our nutrition circumstances for the first year.

I need to pause here to tell you something that took me years to learn and fully let sink in. As I said earlier, I was upset when my boss let me go two weeks before my due date. I also noted that it didn't change that I was covered in God's peace. Consequently, I wasn't worried about it. The truth is this: everyone has a role to play. She met me with kindness and compassion when I lost my mother, never asking for me to reimburse her for the plane ticket she purchased for me to go home that night. That was the role she played in my darkest day, and it brought me light. I don't know why she let me go at that dinner, but I do know that by her doing it, God set me up for an incredible future, complete with my version of "Supermarket Sweep," and for that, I am thankful.

*So, What Now?*

It had been a few weeks since having the baby, and guess who was still without a job? There had been no word following my interview with the company I hoped would be my new employer. Confidently covered in peace and armed with faithful excitement, I accepted my friend's invitation to attend an event Black River was hosting at the Loveless Barn. I don't know what I expected, but I knew that Black River's CEO, Gordon Kerr, would be there, along with his sister, Kim Pegula, and her husband, Terry, who established the record label. I dressed, did my hair and make-up for the first time since having the baby, and drove down to the event.

After walking around and saying hello to the handful of people I knew, I came face-to-face with the CEO.

*"Hi!"* I said.

Surprised, he answered, *"Hello! "What are you doing here?"*

*"I was invited,"* I said.

*"You know you have the job, right?"* He questioned me.

*"No!"* I excitedly yelled back.

*"You do,"* he said. *"Now go home!"*

I thanked Gordon and happily drove home, ecstatic about my new job. Even though I didn't know what my title would be or the salary I'd be making, I knew that it didn't matter because it would be perfect.

*The New Normal*

It wasn't long before my days began to fly faster than ever. I was getting more sleep, and the last of our much-appreciated visitors had gone home. Having people come to stay with me (one at a time) after Evie was born was a lifesaver. Because there were so many times, Steph can attest that I'd be nursing Evie and ask her to hand me something inches out of my reach. Ha-ha, after a while, she'd look at me with "that face" of annoyance, and I'd have to remind myself of how blessed I was to have her with me and try not to be so needy. After all, she couldn't stay forever.

Not long after I found out I was pregnant and had decided to keep the baby, I had a very strategic dinner to plan. My sister Jacky moved to Nashville a few years after I did, and it's been wonderful having her and her family in town. She and her husband have two beautiful children and were settling into life here after moving from Virginia. So, I called Jacky, and we planned a dinner at PF Changs on West End.

"So, do you like it here?" I eventually worked into the conversation.

"Yeah," she said. "Why, do you ask?"

"Well, I wanted to ask if you think you're going to stay here or are still considering moving to another city.

They moved to Nashville because her husband had a job offer from Vanderbilt University, among other prestigious colleges, so it wasn't out of the question in my mind that they could still move.

"No, we're pretty much here." She answered and again asked, "Why."

"Good." I let out a big breath. "Well, I said, I'm going to have a baby."

Jacky chuckled and said, "I figured it was either going to be that you were pregnant or you'd decided to move."

After my big news was out, we continued to talk about my thoughts on my job, how I'd take care of the baby, what I would need, etc. Jacky is always a very realistic and practical thinker, and I've always trusted her and relied on her for advice.

After discussing childcare options after the baby was born, we decided that when it was time for me to return to work, Jacky could help and keep the baby several days during the work week.

March 13th, 2011– "Tomorrow I start a new job, and tonight I witnessed an Evelyn May milestone. This was the first time, during tummy time, that she lifted and turned her head from one side to the other. And she did it twice" – Dawn Delvo's Facebook Wall

My first day was incredible. I was so excited to be at Black River, meet everyone, see my office, and know I was on the path to a new life with my daughter. I had no idea of the blessings God had in store for me. Evie had her first experience backstage at the Grand Ole Opry when she was only seven weeks old (it took me 25 years to get there), and she met the legendary Pam Tillis. I was blessed to work with Pam early in my career in Nashville, so when I saw her and she saw Evie, Pam lit up.

"Can I hold her?" Pam asked.

"Yes!" I quickly replied. May I take a picture?" I knew this was a moment I just had to capture.

Little did I know that we would run into Pam when Evie was about three months old and when Evie was six months old. Pam was a guest artist at the charity event we were attending with our newly signed artist, country music star Craig Morgan, and of course, we documented this moment with another photo. I joked we needed to see her again to round out our first-year photos.

*The New Neighbor*

Until the construction boom in Nashville, my corner apartment had an incredible view of downtown that is now primarily obstructed by "progress." It also has a great view of the parking lot across the street, where the "cool kids" in my building would spend a lot of time hanging out when the weather was nice. There were so many times I'd see them through my window and wonder what they were like or why I wasn't a part of their group.

As Evie and I left my building to go to and from work, I slowly started running into people living there. One of my favorite introductions was with Mike and Katie as I said hello to them in our parking lot one evening.

I was walking towards the door to go home as they were headed out for the night, looking at me with a puzzled expression. I said,

"Hey! Have you guys met my new roommate?"

Mike looked at me confused and said, "Your roommate has a baby?"

I smiled and said, "My roommate is a baby."

Another funny but much more awkward conversation happened when I returned home with the baby. A guy I had briefly dated and who once lived there apparently moved back into the building, and we came home at the same time, meeting at the front door.

"Hey." He said, looking confused.

"Who's that?" He asked.

"I had a baby," I replied.

"When?" He asked, looking even more confused.

I looked down at my little infant and said,

"About a month ago."

The door opened, and we went inside.

*Best Laid Plans*

Some of my best laid plans have failed to work out because God had a different vision in mind. One of those "failed plans" that was instead the gift that keeps on giving is having Evie stay at my sister Jacky's house as an infant when I went to work. Already beyond busy caring for two small children, a husband, and a career, adding a tiny baby into the mix wasn't working out. We both realized this early, and I was beginning to think about alternative childcare options. (Translation: I started to worry about what I would do, who would watch her, and how much it would cost.)

That same week, as I walked towards the exit of my apt building following my lunch break, a very southern and sweet voice called out from the laundry room.

"Hey!" she said.

"I'm a model, but I'm not doing very much. If you ever need anyone to watch the baby, I'd love to."

It was like an angel came straight down from heaven. I told her I'd love to talk about it after work. Beginning in March, when Evie was about two months old, Katie started watching her every day at home. It was perfect because all of Evie's stuff was here, Katie didn't have to travel, and I could come home and see her every day to nurse her at lunch and give Katie a break. No joke, I trusted her completely, and she fell in love with Evie. She would send me photos during the day of what they were doing and even did a little photo shoot outside one day, resulting in one of my favorite early pictures of Evie.

I would have had no way of knowing that Evie would be the one to open so many doors for me. From Katie poking her head out of the laundry room that day and forever becoming a massive part of our lives, to meeting and living life with our incredible neighbors, including Staria and Jordan, my tiny baby elevated my status to being one of "the cool kids" in our building. With that, our first group photo was taken during Black River Studios' reopening of Sound Stage party in June of 2011.

*God Provides*

It's astonishing to think about all that God's provided for us. I already mentioned my fun in the supermarket and with my apartment, but it goes way beyond that.

Around my 3rd trimester, my nephew Charles had outgrown his crib/toddler bed, and my sister Jacky and her family gave me the crib and a matching dresser that doubled as her changing table. Someone donated a fancy Medela breast pump and all the supplies to me. Even my doctor who delivered Evie, who my best friend Mandy nannies for, gave us a big bag full of incredible books and brain-building toys. And the clothes, so many bags of clothes, beautiful clothes. Let me tell you, from strangers to family and friends, that cup overflowed. To this day, years later, we are still being blessed with clothes to the point that I can tell you that I've only had to buy Evie a handful of clothing items, mostly because I was in a pinch on our way somewhere and we forgot something or had a spill, etc. Thankfully, I was able to nurse Evie for six months exclusively and continued to nurse her until she turned one. Towards the end of that first year, when the stockpile of frozen liquid gold was running low, I was again blessed. A friend of a friend within the music community gave us a case of liquid baby formula because her new baby didn't take to it. On top of those physical blessings are the countless thoughts, love, and prayers we received.

Do you know what? I think prayers are more valuable than any gifts. A year ago or so, I was listening to a speaker who recommended that parents read Mark Batterson's book *Praying Circles Around Your Children*. In the book, he writes, "The greatest legacy you can leave your children are your prayers because they continue to work even after you pass on." As a woman who's lost her mother and now IS a mother, that affected me.

I shared that sentiment with a girlfriend on the phone one night as we were wrapping up a texting conversation that ran very late. Faithe has a son a few years younger than Evie, and we had just talked about sneaking into our babies' rooms and kissing them before we turned in for the night. I told her that every night I pray over Evie, "May she grow in wisdom and stature and in favor with God and with man to be like a woman of Proverbs 31." I took the first part of that prayer from Mark Batterson's book and added the Proverbs 31 line because that's still something I'm working towards.

I told Faithe that Batterson explains that prayers for your child, or anyone, live on even after the one who prays that prayer passes. In an unexpected response, Faithe asked me my mom's name.

I answered her, "Her name was Barb."

"Well," she said, "tonight in my prayers, I'll pray that Barb's prayers take an extra lap around you and Evie." That was one of the most moving and powerful things anyone has ever said to me, and I burst into tears.

Those early days at Black River are precious to think back on because I genuinely stepped into a new life. The life I had always dreamed of but never knew what it would be like to live. I remember going to work so excitedly. What I'm about to say might sound bad, but going to work after having an infant at home for weeks now felt like a mini vacation. At least mentally. I could leave the room without fear of someone needing me immediately, and I could go and get coffee if I wanted, or I could go to the bathroom without worrying about a baby crying or needing to bring her with me. It was a place where I could just be myself, and I began to discover who that was.

Another incredible thing about being at Black River was that although I had, and loved, that separation for a few hours a day, I also had the freedom to have her with me if needed. Some of my most fond memories of those early days include her strapped to my chest while I was working at my desk or hanging in a bouncy swing from my office doorway. One of those days, Evie was with me for whatever reason, and she was crying in my office, and I couldn't get her to stop. I felt terrible, and people were working. They needed to be having phone conversations, and here I was with a crying baby. Then I saw a note slide under my door. I remember feeling nervous. "Well, there it is. I'm going to get kicked out," I thought. I couldn't have been more wrong. It was from my CEO, Gordon Kerr, and it simply read, "Can I hold her?"

I didn't know it then because I was too mortified to say yes, but he meant it.

Another of my favorite early office moments was with Rachael, our Promotion Coordinator. I was in her office, letting her know I was thinking about heading home because it was getting late, and I wanted to get Ev down for a nap. Ev was nestled on my chest very sweetly while I talked to her, and then it happened. She threw up on me in Rachael's office so hard I didn't even know what to do. Rachael lost it laughing at me, and I just stood there, covered. Thankfully, I took the brunt of it, and nothing fell to the ground. I looked at Rachael and said, "Actually, I think I'll just go now." She helped me leave the office, and I drove the 2 minutes home without a seatbelt, so my car didn't stink for seven years. My poor baby was sick because she was so congested from allergies that she was choking on the drainage. I peeled off her clothes and started a bath for her. As I was walking from her room to the bathroom, she threw up on me again. I was caught off guard and felt a little defeated, but not mad, and I just felt bad for my sweet girl. Once I got her in the bathroom and stripped off my disgusting clothes, I knew we were on the right path. She was in her tub for about one minute before she pooped in it.

You can't make this stuff up. I just started laughing and started over.

Thankfully, during those first few weeks, I had a lot of help. Stephanie and Jacky were there when Evie was born, and Steph stayed for about two weeks. My dear friend Fish came to see me shortly after with her sweet boy, Sebastian. My sister Kristy visited after that, and I am incredibly thankful for everyone who helped in those early days. Every single changed diaper, bath time, cuddle, and kiss Evelyn received were blessings from God. I don't think I could have held it all together, and I definitely had my moments where I didn't, but overall, they helped me give Evelyn the best start I possibly could because they let me sleep or go to Starbucks by myself for a moment of alone time. I didn't want to get away. I just needed a couple more moments to prepare for my new life, which now revolved around my daughter's well-being.

While Kristy was in Nashville, we talked about our mom and how much we missed her. It is still hard to believe she's gone and that she's not here to meet my baby or several of her new grandchildren. Kristy told me that she still talks to her out loud. That sounded weird to me because I don't believe she's always listening. I honestly hope she's not listening; that doesn't seem very peaceful. However, I believe I can talk to Jesus, and He can pass on a message or give me one.

Around that time, Gordon's sister and brother-in-law, Kim and Terry Pegula, bought the Buffalo Sabres, and there was a lot of hockey talk at Black River. I went to bed one night and had my first dream about my mom. In the dream, I was playing hockey and was in the middle of a game. All of a sudden, my mom was on the outside of the rink, yelling at me to get my attention.

"Dawn!" I just kept playing, even though I heard her. I was embarrassed but primarily frustrated at the distraction.

"Dawn!?" she called out again.

"Mom!" I answered, yelling back. "I can't talk to you right now. I'm playing hockey!"

Then, with her right next to me, almost in a whisper, she said, "Just because you're playing hockey doesn't mean you can't talk to me." I took that as a sign that I could try to talk to her or at least send Jesus messages to pass along to her.


*Child Support or Naw?*

One question I used to get all the time, and still do today, is, "Is her dad involved?" or "Do you get child support?" It's so funny because the whole time I was pregnant, I would think, "Surely he'll come around before the baby is born. I know it wasn't in our plan, but he'll come around." Then she was born, and he didn't. Then I thought he'd surely come around before she turned one, two, three… he didn't.

So many people wanted me to file for child support, but it didn't feel right to me. He was too angry, too mean, and too unpredictable. He knows where I live, and I have a dark parking lot. I didn't want to look over my shoulder every night, worrying about who might be lurking. Did you know that the majority of deaths in pregnant women are at the hands of the baby's father? I knew, and it was on my mind every night I came home from work before she was born.

My natural instinct has always been to protect my baby. From the night I accepted the pregnancy as a gift from God and slept with a pillow between me and the edge of my bed, as if I'd suddenly fall out of bed for the first time in 25 years, to my not wanting to further anger him by filing for child support. I didn't want "hate mail" in the form of a monthly check. I didn't want someone in our life who didn't want to be there. Most importantly, we were not in need. God was giving us everything we needed and more, and I just had to keep trusting in Him.

There's also the legal issue. For me to get child support, I'd have to establish him as her father, and child support opens the door to visitation and possibly even grandparents' rights. I'm all about family, but here's the thing: he never told his family. They don't know about the most precious grandbaby, niece, or cousin; that is, their family. I thought, "I can't open up that part of his world, but I'm open to him doing it."

## *New Car Smell*

After several months of living with my new "roommate," I strongly felt it was time to get a new car. My current 2002 Hyundai Sonata had over 100,000 miles, and although it was a good car, I felt like I needed something newer, bigger, and more reliable to protect my six-month-old daughter. This wasn't the first time I decided to upgrade vehicles, and the idea of getting a new car, or more significantly, the thought of saying goodbye to my current car, was a bittersweet concept.

I decided I needed a new car when I graduated from high school. So I went down to the Hyundai dealership, got a loan, and drove away with a brand new 2000 Hyundai Sonata. It was silver and beautiful, and I loved it, especially the door handles. Sad, but true. I remember driving away thinking, "Wow. What did I do? I just bought a brand-new car! Holy moly."

A few years later, I was home from college, and my parents borrowed my car to go to the nearby casino. It wasn't unusual for them to borrow it; they were known to frequent the casino, and my car was the newest and most comfortable ride. My mom and dad were not drinkers, and I had no reason to say no. I wish I had needed it, though.

The next morning, I went upstairs to the living room and sat on the couch as usual. Soon afterward, I was playing with my niece Jaida, a toddler at the time, and my parents entered the room. Dad handed me the keys and said, "Here's what's left of your car." Ha. Right? That's the joke people often make after borrowing someone's car. This time, though, it was no joke. My car was totaled, and the consequences have been far-reaching.

Early that morning, a fog set in as they were driving home. There is a hill on that two-lane stretch of highway connecting Prairie Knights Casino to Mandan, North Dakota, and hidden in the fog at the bottom of it was an unoccupied car on their side of the road. My parents crashed into the non-moving vehicle with intense force. The good-intentioned driver of the car was an employee of the casino. He abandoned his vehicle on the road to go into the ditch and check on a person he saw there, apparently passed out. Thankfully, no harm came to either of those men, but unfortunately, my parents hit his car head-on with little time to react due to the dense fog. My mom was the most severely injured and would experience back and full body pains for years to come.

My parents filed a lawsuit and received a settlement, and with that, I came home one day to a new car — a beautiful blue Hyundai Sonata, this time with a sunroof. I remember how I felt driving it for the first time because it was so beautiful, and I was incredibly thankful. That car had a lot of sentimental value because it was given to me by my parents, and now my mom was gone.

Evelyn and I went to the dealership after work one day, and I was determined. After an hour or more of searching, I decided upon a silver 2010 Santa Fe. My financial situation wasn't great coming out of my previous several years at a low-paying job, and my credit score was also lacking. Consequently, I had to go with the dealership's financing option, which I'm ashamed to say was nearly 15% interest. It was in my head that I needed that car, and that's what would happen. After I completed the paperwork, I went out to my memory-laden Hyundai Sonata, including the floor mats from my original Sonata that I jacked from the scrap yard when my dad took me there to say goodbye to it, packed up my belongings, and left it there.

That night, I drove the 15 miles home in awe and a little overwhelmed. I can still see the blue lights from the interior gauges lighting up my face as I look in the rearview mirror at my sleeping baby. "Oh my God," I thought. "I'm a mom and just bought a new car."

*A Simple Invitation*

I felt a powerful urge to attend church when Evie was old enough to leave the house. I'd wanted to find a church home in Nashville for quite a while, but I'd never done it. Being raised Catholic, looking for a local Catholic church was the natural place for me to start looking for a new church home. I researched Catholic churches in the area and began attending a new one each weekend. We went to several churches, but nothing felt right to me. I hate to say it, but I didn't feel welcome. Sometimes, we'd come and go through the entire service without anyone saying a word to us. Overall, I felt like the "unmarried sinner" who had an out-of-wedlock baby, who should be quiet. Granted, I'm sure that was me internalizing my issues at the time while dealing with "Ben's" total dismissal, but again, that's how I was feeling.

Frustrated with the results, I planned to continue the search until one day when I experienced a very important

*God Splice*[1] while I was in the conference room at Black River. I was wrapping up a meeting with our CEO, Gordon Kerr, when, for some reason, we began discussing the possibility of our building being haunted.

"Do you think it's haunted?" Gordon asked. "Me? No, I don't think so." I answered. Granted, I hadn't been there for very long then, but I had spent time there alone.

"I've been here alone at night and never felt anything weird." I continued. "And I've been in other places at night and absolutely felt uncomfortable and haunted."

"It's interesting you brought up coming here at night and not feeling scared in the dark," Gordon said. "Our pastor was just preaching about light cutting into the darkness in the sermon this weekend."

I found this very interesting, and we talked about my lackluster mission to find us a new church home.

"You should come to check out Brentwood Baptist with us this weekend. Mike Glenn is incredible."

"Okay, we will!" I answered.

### *1st trip to* ND

Taking Evelyn home to North Dakota was an incredible experience. She's the person I love the most in this world, and I got to take her home to the people who made me who I am. She met her cousin Cooper, who is just six months younger than her, and to this day, people ask if they are twins. Evelyn met her Uncle Matt and her cousins Jaida and Sami. They all welcomed her with open

---

[1] *The God Splice,* Written by Gordon S. Kerr

arms and are now more like siblings than cousins in many ways.

She met my dear Grandma T in Texas when we visited for my cousin's wedding, and I'll never forget how happy I was seeing her hold my sweet baby for the first time. When we were together again in North Dakota, I took a photo of my grandma's delicate fingers holding Evelyn's tiny new toes, and it's everything.

My dad watched Evelyn and me play on the floor in the living room one day. She was lying there cooing on her back, and I gazed into her face, laughing and taking in the moment. He said, "I hope you always do that; get down to her level." We still have moments like that every night when I tuck her in and again when I wake her up in the morning.

*A Time to Crawl*

When Evie was about nine months old, we were blessed to be back at the Grand Ole Opry to see one of our artists perform. Not knowing any better, I brought Evie with me. She was getting to the point where I knew she would start crawling, and that night seemed the perfect night to do it. So, I set her down backstage on the newly remodeled, beautiful hardwood floor with a guitar pick-shaped Grand Ole Opry logo, and I crossed my fingers that she'd crawl. Evie looked up at me with the most beautiful little face, started to move back and forth, and then, nothing. Well, nothing except for this her happy sweet face and some great photos.

*The First Time, For Me*

I love my job, and I've enjoyed it from the first day I stepped foot into the offices on Music Row. It had always been my dream to work in a place like Black River, and back then, I was so happy to have my foot in the door officially! I was home with Evie for about eight weeks before returning to work, and I loved my time at home with her. When I began working, however, I realized the time away from her was a much-needed break, almost like a mini vacation, that revitalized me and allowed me to return to her with a happy heart. I missed her while working, and sometimes people would tell me to "stop rocking" while I was in the office without her. I unconsciously made the motion my body was accustomed to while caring for my infant.

Thankfully, I was promoted early at Black River to run in-house publicity, which meant I could travel with our artists and continue building and developing relationships with the media. Working 40 hours a week and adding to that a travel schedule, I knew I'd be spending more time away from my sweet baby girl—the months in that first year flew by almost as fast as their milestones.

Just after I had Evelyn with me at the Grand Ole Opry at nine months old, I knew she would be crawling at any second. I had a work trip to NYC the next week and was so scared I would miss it. I saw her pull herself up for one of the first times on a video Katie sent me while I was away, and I figured I'd see her crawl for the first time on a video, too.

With new crawling news coming in soon, I picked her up from Katie when I returned to town and took my sweet girl to the park for some mama-daughter time. On the cushy playground, I sat her down there and marveled at God's creation. Just then, I decided to toss my keys a bit in front of her. She looked at me with a wild, beautiful smile, then slowly crawled to the keys. It was an incredible moment, and I was so proud of her and so happy to be her mom.

Even at that moment, happy as I was, it's reasonable to assume that she probably crawled some while I was on the road and she was with Katie. Nevertheless, I am so thankful that I don't know that to be true because it taught me a precious lesson:

I may miss her first time crawling, her first steps, her first word. For all we know, she could do all those things in bed while I'm asleep. The point is she will crawl, walk, and speak. When I see it, it will be for the first time, for me.

That brought me a lot of peace, and I hope it brings others peace, too, because we can't be in all places at all times. We are not God, but God knows that and blesses us with those moments in His time.

*Oh, Mandy*

A few weeks before Evie turned one, my friend Mandy had an event where Evie's dad worked. She went with her husband and knew "Ben" worked there, so upon arrival, she asked if he was there. They told her no and asked if there was anything they could do to help her. Mandy said, "No, it's a good thing he's not here, or I'd punch him in the face." Not a normal response, I'm sure. The man looked at her funny and asked why. She said, "He just had a baby with my friend and won't fess up to it." Then, the man replied simply, "That sounds about right."

Mandy went into the event and called me immediately to tell me about it, still shaking. I said to her, "Wow. If he were a girl, I'd give him 10 minutes before this gets back to me. Since he's a dude, I'll give it 20."

I was thankful to have such an incredible friend who would stand up for Evie, and I liked that, but I didn't want trouble. He had not warmed up to the idea of being a father in the last almost two years since finding out he would be one, and I didn't think this would melt his heart by any means.

About 10 minutes later, the text messages started coming in, and he was livid.

"Don't you ever send anyone to my work! You are ruining my life…" I told him I didn't know what he was talking about and didn't send anyone anywhere. "I'm a little busy taking care of things here to worry about you or your work." He continued to tell me that if I ever sent anyone to his work again, "Someone would get hurt."

That was not happening. I said, "Listen, you son of a bitch, if you ever threaten me or my daughter again, you will have a restraining order slapped on your ass so fast, you won't even be out of bed tomorrow." It still makes my blood boil to think about it even now.

He texted back, "Just leave me alone." That's such a sad message in one line.

Although that was a time of conflict, and I could have easily been upset with Mandy for rocking the boat, I'm thankful, and not surprised, that she did. Mandy and I have been friends since I moved to Nashville, and she has an incredible heart. She has been a prayer warrior for me, even enlisting her mom to help sometimes! When my mom passed away in 2009, Mandy was continually checking on me and showering me with love and support. I was in North Dakota for about a month after losing my mom, and I doubt if a day went by without getting some message or call from her. Not too long after, Mandy lost her father, and I tried my best to be there for her in a similar fashion. Losing a parent is so hard. It's the kind of grief that cuts so intensely it can open right back up and hurt as if you are back in that moment at any given time. I'm sad to say that I didn't attend her father's funeral in New Orleans. I knew how much I was empathizing and crying for her here in Nashville, still reeling from the loss of my mother, that I'd be a blubbering mess. I wouldn't bring her much comfort in those dark moments if I couldn't keep myself together to be strong for her. So, instead of attending, I prayed and prayed for her. I'd check in and remember her on the sad days, just as she does for me. It is a huge responsibility to love someone and genuinely care for them in good times and bad times. Mandy has shown me what that looks like, and I'm forever thankful to her for that.

## *A Measure of Time*

I once posted a photo on Instagram to let some friends in England know I'll be going to the UK in a few weeks and wanted to see them. Looking at the picture of us, it didn't feel like a million years ago until I got to the hashtag. It was 17 years ago. Oh, my goodness. I know just by writing the word hashtag, I outdated this book before it's even been read for edits, most likely, but that's my point. Time can go so fast.

When Evie was a baby, I'd read her *Goodnight Moon* before bed; it was a precious moment I could count on every night. What I didn't count on was how quickly and how often I found myself reading *Goodnight Moon*. It was Groundhog Day, and I could feel time slipping through my fingers with the whisper of "goodnight noises everywhere." It was one of those nights when I remember Evie rubbing my arm with her tiny hand, on purpose, for the first time. It was heaven-sent.

Another thing about time is that it comes. There's a time for everything, and one of those times was when our precious nanny, Katie, knew the time had come for her to leave Nashville and move home to Oklahoma. Of course, that timing was terrible for me because it was right before a very busy CMA Music Festival that I was counting on her to keep Evie through.

When I realized something was wrong and she was leaving, we went downstairs and had a group cry, and then she left.

## A Time to Shine

Excited about my promotion, I was empowered to dream big and develop ideas to help our artists reach the next level. I remember brainstorming about Craig Morgan's upcoming album in a meeting one day, and a seemingly crazy idea came flying out of my mouth, "I could get Craig on *Army Wives*." Everyone in the room looked at me like I had a third head. "It makes sense," I continued. "With his military background and the music on this album. I know someone who works does the music on the show." "Okay," the collective room said, "Go get *Army Wives*." Looking back, that was a hilarious moment because most of the people in that room had been working in the music industry for much longer than I had, and this was not a typical get. In fact, I don't know that they'd had any country music artists on the show. Thankfully, I didn't realize that and wasn't worried about failing. Given the opportunity and God's help, I can make incredible things fall into place, so I went for it.

When I returned to my office, I started planning the pitch to Marianne, the VP of Music at Lifetime Television, an incredible lady I've already mentioned. Looking back now, I realized for the very first time that it was God's hand that moved for us to get *Army Wives*.

True to her encouraging words that day I told her I was expecting, Marianne reached out to me via email entitled, "Checking In…" in September of 2010. She was writing to check on me; at the time, I was five months pregnant and still working for my former employer and wrote:

"Hi Dawn, I just came across your name in my email folder and thought I'd check in on you to see how you're doing, how your precious 'work in progress' is coming along, and to say hi!"

Remembering her incredible love and support, I walked into my meeting that day, and the idea of *Army Wives* came out of my mouth. Little did I know that in October of 2011, we'd be confirmed to go to Charleston, South Carolina, and tape an episode that featured Craig not only as a performer on the popular television show but as an actor, written into the script for that episode. Booking Craig Morgan on *Army Wives* has been and always will be one of my most significant career achievements. It's because of God and keeping good relationships with incredible people.

# MILESTONES AND MISHAPS 2012



*Evie's 1st Birthday*

People often say time flies, but I don't think it sinks in until you're a parent. I waited and waited and waited for Evie to be born, and then there I was, about to celebrate her first birthday in January 2012. Before she was born, I called her my little ladybug. I can't remember why, but I had her bedroom all decorated with ladybugs. The theme continued through to her first birthday and beyond.

When planning her birthday, people told me the first birthday is more for the parents than the baby, so you can make it more catered to adults. I didn't have enough space at home to host many people for this party, so I asked Gordon if I could do it at Black River. My father was flying into Nashville for her birthday, which was a big deal because my dad hadn't been to visit us in Nashville yet. In fact, he hadn't been to Nashville since my mom passed away in 2009.

Thankfully, Dad got on a plane and made it to Tennessee in one piece. I remember posting on Facebook the night he arrived that I had him all tucked in, safely watching some Western on TV.

That Saturday, Dad helped me load up my car and take Evie the few blocks to Black River Entertainment to set up for her birthday party. Not only did Gordon allow us to use the label's spacious "family room" for the party, but he also gifted us the food.

God brought so many people into our lives to walk with us that first year and beyond. The cool kids from the parking lot, the friends from our new church, Gordon and Kim, Evie's nanny Katie and her boyfriend Jimmy, my original Nashville family from my very first summer in town, my sister and her family, the neighborhood families, and my dad.

It was fun having so many incredibly important people to us gathered in one place, and before we got to the cake and the presents, I knew I needed to take a moment and say thank you. It's been a few years since this moment, but it went something like this. "Hello, everyone. I want to take a minute to say thank you before we cut the cake. (Tears began to form in my eyes then and are streaming down my face as I write this now.) There are so many of you here to celebrate with us today, my dad included, and I want you all to know that you're here because of how special you are to us. We didn't make it to a year alone, and we made it to this day because all of you have been with us, making today possible." Naturally, I started to cry during that little speech, not the ugly horse cry noise I made at my baby shower back in North Dakota in front of my family when I was thanking them for being there and reflecting on my mom not being three, but a decent ugly cry just the same.

I could feel the Holy Spirit in that room as I looked around at all of God's blessings, and there was so much joy; it brings me to tears again now. The lady who made the ladybug cake documented it in her blog, 52 Weeks of Sweets, and you can see Evie's first tastes right here.

### The "Nice" Text

Once I knew my journey included having a baby and decided to take on that role as a solo parent, I always thought, "He'll come around. Unexpectedly, becoming a father is not easy news to process, but once she's born, he'll come around."

If you remember from a few pages back, my previous dialogue with Evie's dad came a few before her birthday when my friend Mandy had an event where he worked and asked one of his co-workers if he was there. That was not a favorable exchange, although I held my ground with him and still stand by everything I said.

A week or two after her 1st birthday, he texted me out of the blue and said, "I'm not ready and won't be for a while, but happy first year."

Shocked, I asked him, "Is this your way to mess with me while I'm at work?"

"No, he said. "Don't text back; I'm just being nice." Being nice, ha. I don't like being told what to do, so I texted back. We had a few exchanges over the first year, but this was the most positive conversation, and it still makes me sad. That was the last time he contacted me; he still has never asked about her or how she's doing.

### Where Am I Going to Be?

Once Katie left to return to Oklahoma, it was time to find new childcare for Evie. While I loved the idea of having her at home and near me, the care I was receiving wasn't a good fit, and I began looking for alternatives I could afford. Eventually, I got her into a beautiful facility in downtown Nashville. It was perfect on paper and close to both my office and home. I'd drop her off and feel good about where she would spend her day. They would send home little notes to tell me what she ate, how she played, and if she said anything cute or funny that day. I also loved the art projects they'd do because they incorporated her little hands and feet in artwork and dated them on special holidays like Mother's Day or Valentine's Day. Unfortunately, with daycare came other kids' germs and sicknesses. I had to pick her up often and then her not being allowed back for a day or two, which meant I still had to pay them and also needed someone to stay home with her or I had to miss work. That was getting very stressful and expensive. Additionally, she began to have issues with other children biting her on her arm. "What? Someone bit my BABY?" I was furious because it happened several times, and I'm talking teeth marks that left significant bruising and light breaking of the skin. I began to feel terrible and trapped. Here I was, paying top dollar for this "perfect" place, causing us much stress.

One morning, after I dropped her off, one of the teachers pulled me aside to talk about my one-year-old. She told me she wondered if this was the right place for Evelyn. (Now, mind you, I'm already thinking this, but to hear some woman tell me that she didn't think Evie was right for this place was about to light a fuse in me.) She said that Evie didn't participate, didn't smile, or have fun there. She said, "Evie will sit on a chair holding her blanket and bunny and rock. That ticked me off. I'm paying these people a lot to care for my daughter. Why weren't they interacting with her? The lady directed me to the TV monitor so I could see into the playroom, and she was sitting in a corner by herself, holding her lovie. So, I asked her, "Why does she have her blanket and bunny? That is only for nap time; she should put it away and play with people." She looked at me blankly, and I went back into the room. I walked up to Evie, lovingly put her blanket and bunny back into her cubby, directed her to a play area, kissed her, and left the room. I watched her a minute longer as she continued to play, and then I left, very upset and feeling even more like I was failing my baby. Evie is a HAPPY baby; she only fusses when she needs something, and what this woman told me made it sound like Evie was depressed. I needed help and didn't know what to do. Thankfully, God already had a plan.

Shortly after that day at preschool, I was at my sister Jacky's house, and her neighbor Melissa came over, which was not unusual because the whole neighborhood was very close.

We were chatting, and she asked me, "Hey, would you ever consider taking Evie out of school and letting me keep her?"

Melissa had taught preschool for many years prior and was excellent with children. She was someone I initially hoped would keep Evie for me, but she specializes in preschool-age, not infants.

"Um, would I!?" I thought.

"Yes, thank you! That would be amazing!"

Melissa and Evie were together on weekdays for several years before I enrolled her in preschool. I owe so much to Melissa for the time and love she poured into Evie's early years, teaching and nourishing her in ways I couldn't have imagined. I'm equally thankful to my sister, Jacky, for continuing to be a connector and supporter of our family. It does take a village to raise a child, and I am beyond thankful for these two ladies with their open doors and hearts. For those couple of years, I picked up my sweet, happy baby every day, likely covered in dirt from playing outside and beat from a fun day of just being a kid. It was an answered prayer every day.

And Katie? She moved home to Oklahoma, started school, and fell in love. Not only did she fall in love, but she also fell in love with her best friend from second grade. They are married now and just had their first child. Evie was the flower girl. Don't tell us that God doesn't have a plan for us all.

*The Letters*

Later that year, I saw the news on Facebook about someone unexpectedly passing away, and naturally, that made me very sad. Shortly after that, my great Aunt Evelyn passed away, and it got me thinking about people who say things like, "If only I had the chance to say…" or "I wish I would have told him/her that I…" and it made me mad. We have the chance to say or do something with every breath we breathe. So, I asked myself, "Who are the people that, if they passed away today, you would say this about?" I came up with the same two people I needed to tell I was having a baby before I shared the news with the rest of my world: Dad and Grandma. That night, I sat down and wrote a letter to my grandma. It was two or three pages of how much she means to me and how much she continues to influence my life. I included my earliest memories of spending time at her home and church and thanked her for being my first stable display of continued faith in Jesus. I spilled my heart on her in those pages, and I said everything I'd ever wanted to tell her, and I'm so thankful that I did. I mailed it and heard back from her a couple of weeks later, and now my heart is happy and at peace.

The same goes for Dad. I treasure him so much, but I don't remember ever really expressing that past the "I love you(s)" and "thank you(s)." I can confidently say he knows how much he means to me on any given day.

*Second Dream About Mom*

Things were going well for me at work and home. Evie was a happy baby, and she was growing so much! She had been crawling for some time and began to start walking. As my tiny baby grew up, I thought I'd miss much of what she's outgrown. In God's goodness, every phase she grows into comes with so much joy that it outshines the past moments, and my heart keeps filling up. It's interesting to feel that way now as I begin to understand what it means to be a mother, especially when my mother is gone. I would have loved to tell my mom, "I get it now," or "Thank you for not giving up on me when I treated you terribly as a grumpy teenager."

One night, after a stressful but not too-bad few days of work, I fell asleep and had a "work dream." Thankfully,

I am now working in the career that I love and am super passionate about, so work dreams are not near the nightmare that waitressing dreams used to be! In this dream, a co-worker and I were looking for Craig Morgan's cabin. I believe I was looking for his cabin because since I grew up with a cabin and to this day miss it so much, Craig and I had talked about his and that they may have plans to sell it. Anyway, Rachael and I were looking all over the place, on the water, around the lakeshore, and could not find his cabin. Suddenly, I'm back at the Black River offices, standing by an elevator, which we don't have in real life, and I'm tired, frustrated, and mentally and physically exhausted. Just then, my mom approached me and said, "Hi, what's wrong?" I looked at her and explained the situation. "I'm trying to find Craig Morgan's cabin; I've looked all over the place, but I can't find him or the cabin, and I just really, REALLY need a hug from you right now. She pulled me into one of her cherished "mom hugs" and said, "Anywhere, anytime." I felt every moment of that dream; it was real, and I'll never forget it.

*Staying Humble*

With highs come lows. It's the natural order, keeping things balanced, I suppose. Things had been going so well then, and I was thriving (in my opinion) as a mom and in my new role at Black River.

Returning to the idea of balance, with all of the good came elements and opportunities for bad. Living life and working in the music industry has always been my dream, however, there was no way of knowing what it would entail.

Outside of the music, famous people, red carpets, private planes (honestly, I've only flown privately for work three times. Still, check that box!), fabulous work trip travel, and Delta Sky Miles, there are long hours, time away from my sweet baby, egos, high-stress levels, tempting situations and alcohol. Lots and lots and lots of alcohol. Fortunately for me, alcohol is the extent of what I've ever witnessed in Country Music. It's not like you must have a drink every hour on the hour, but it seems always to be readily available and often free. During times of celebration like award shows and after parties or at concerts while we're hosting VIPs in the music and media industry, it's effortless to drink, and sometimes to drink too much.

Someone introduced me to the concept of teachable moments early on at Black River, and I often refer to it. When someone in my department or myself makes a mistake that could have "been bad" but turns out to be okay, we use that moment as a "teaching moment." However, it still needs correcting by adequately explaining why it was a wrong choice and what the consequences could have been had things gone south.

My first actual teaching moment at Black River came in April of 2012 while I was in Las Vegas, NV, for the ACM awards. I had traveled to Vegas several times before for the ACM Awards to network and spend time with friends in the music industry, but this was my first time attending the awards for work. I was incredibly excited to walk with my artist and his independent publicist down the ACM red carpet. I was with my Black River team at the radio remotes a day or two before the awards when I received word that I would not be allowed to walk the carpet that year because we had too many people. I was crushed, "visibly crushed," as a kindhearted person pointed it out in the email she forwarded me, sharing the rules of the red carpet for that year. All I could think was, "Why am I even here? Experiencing the red carpet and meeting the attending media was literally the reason I came out here. Now I have no official role or job to do here." Keep in mind that's not true, and I am very narrow-minded. I know that now. I was distraught, defeated, and without a purpose at that moment.

A saving grace at that moment, at least for my heart, was having Evelyn with me in Vegas. Sadly, Katie had moved away by this point but did agree to meet us in Vegas. I was thrilled to have them both there, as the split was sudden and quite sad. Knowing they were upstairs, I went back to my room and spent time loving on my girl.

That night, I did what I had known to do in years past. I pulled myself together and spent the evening networking with friends and having drinks.

### A Sign of the Times

In August of 2012, Katie came back to Nashville for a visit. I was working, so Katie and Evie had some one-on-one time together. They missed each other very much. Later, Katie and I took Evie to the park, to breakfast one day and lunch on another. It's hard to explain how much love and peace Katie brought to our lives while caring for

Evie that first year. God knew what he was doing with that one, and I am incredibly thankful.

While preparing to become a mother, I did a lot of reading and research about babies. One of the things I found to be fascinating is baby sign language. I suppose it's merely sign language, but this use of sign language is specifically for babies that can hear and understand you; they just can't talk yet. I loved the idea and posted a chart of all the top baby signs I wanted to use with Evie. Mostly the basics: milk, eat, all done, more, please, and thank you. Eventually, we added change (diaper change) and swing, and I love you. I'd use these signs every time I said the word or asked her if she wanted one of those items. Katie supported me in this effort and reinforced it by using sign language with her during the day. Something incredible happens between a parent and a child when, before they can speak, they can tell you, crystal clear, what they want. There is no confusion; they say more, eat, milk, all done, etc., and then I would respect and honor her decision as best I could. It alleviated a lot of frustration, and from a very early age, it built trust between us.

We caught some of my favorite moments of Evie's signing on video, and it still warms my heart. Baby sign language is relatively easy to do and teach a baby, so if this interests you, I'd highly encourage it. To this day, Evie sometimes signs in an excited moment, and I can quickly remind her to say thank you without ever speaking a word that may embarrass her.

*Pastors at Brentwood Baptist*

Since Gordon's invitation to check out Brentwood Baptist Church, Evie and I became regular attendees. My first impressions were very surface-level. I loved the feel of the building. BBC is a massive structure located at 777 Concord Road in Brentwood, Tenn., but Hudson Hall, where we attended the 11:11 am church service on Sunday mornings, was very intimate. It looks like a medium-sized auditorium with a back wall of bleacher seating and several rows of chairs in front that lead to many circular tables reaching the stage. Every morning, I would walk in, greet the Kerrs, hand off Evie to Ms. Kim for some snuggle time, and then grab a cup of coffee before the service started. It was a beautiful routine. The church service usually opens with three contemporary Christian songs performed by a stellar band and, at that time, a woman named Ashley. This woman took me to a place with her singing, and she was so powerful, so moving, and so beautiful that the music opened my heart, head, and often tear ducts, preparing me for the worship service ahead.

Growing up Catholic, I have been to more church services than I could even begin to count, but these were not like any other from my past. Mike Glenn, the senior pastor at BBC, cut through every wall or resistance I had developed over the years, and I swear he spoke directly to me every Sunday. He has a way of teaching from the Bible and incorporating our modern-day life events and challenges like I've never heard before. Similarly, he'd read a passage from the Bible that I've glazed over a time or two and explain it in a way that made it new. He makes the people in the Bible, people I can relate to, empathize with, or honestly, sometimes he'll point out their mistakes and how God still used them in a way that makes me feel less stupid or that there's hope for me yet! Most Sundays, at some point, I end up crying. Sometimes, I don't know why; other times, it's obvious. I don't understand why Brentwood Baptist Church became my home in 2011; perhaps my heart was ready in a way that it had never been before. My attention span may have grown. Or maybe I just needed to be filled up with the good news of Jesus. Whatever the reason, that decision changed my life, and I'm thankful.

Aaron Bryant is another pastor at the church who significantly impacted me in the early days. If Mike Glenn looks like Steve Martin, and he does, Aaron looks like an admirable opponent on one of the toughest college football teams. Very tall, with broad shoulders and a strong stance, Aaron now cuts through a different kind of defensive line, the ones surrounding our hearts.

One Sunday, as I was holding my little baby butt nestled under my chin, Aaron began to preach about King David. I'm not a theologian and won't pretend to be, so I will explain this as I took it to mean. Aaron was preaching about King David and his struggles with sin as they related to lust, temptation, and jealousy. He explained that even though David was a King, anointed by God, he struggled. He was human, and it became effortless to relate to David. I saw him in a new light, making it easier to identify with him. It was all too easy, as it turned out.

The reading is from **2 Samuel 11:2-5** David's Adultery with Bathsheba.

*"In the spring when kings march out to war, David sent Joab with his officers and all Israel. They destroyed the Ammonites and besieged Rabbah, but David remained in Jerusalem."*

*One evening David got up from his bed and strolled around on the roof of the palace. From the roof he saw a woman bathing — a very beautiful woman. So, David sent someone to inquire about her, and he said, "Isn't this Bathsheba, daughter of Eliam and wife of Uriah the Hethite?" David sent messengers to get her, and when she came to him, he slept with her. Now, she had just been purifying herself from her uncleanness. Afterward, she returned home. The woman conceived and sent word to inform David: "I am pregnant."*

*Aaron taught us about David's actions after finding out she was pregnant. David immediately tried to cover his tracks by sending for her husband to come home, hoping he would sleep with his wife and think the baby was his.*

### *From 2 Samuel 11:6-13*

*"David sent orders to Joab: "Send me Uriah the Hethite." So Joab sent Uriah to David. When Uriah came to him, David asked how Joab and the troops were doing and how the war was going. Then he said to Uriah, "Go down to your house and wash your feet." So Uriah left the palace, and a gift from the king followed him. But Uriah slept at the door of the palace with all his master's servants; he did not go down to his house. When it was reported to David, "Uriah didn't go home," David questioned Uriah, "Haven't you just come from a journey? Why didn't you go home?" Uriah answered David, "The ark, Israel, and Judah are dwelling in tents, and my master Joab and his soldiers are camping in the open field.*

*How can I enter my house to eat and drink and sleep with my wife? As surely as you live and by your life, I will not do this!" "Stay here today also," David said to Uriah, "and tomorrow I will send you back." So, Uriah stayed in Jerusalem that day and the next. Then David invited Uriah to eat and drink with him, and David got him drunk. He went out in the evening to lie down on his cot with his master's servants, but he did not go home."*

Although Uriah did come home, David's plan did not work because Uriah never entered his home as not to dishonor his God, country and yes, his King. The next day, David tried to trick him into going home and sleeping with his wife by getting him drunk. He failed again. Feeling as though he had no other options, David plotted the unthinkable.

### Uriah's Death Arranged 2 Samuel 11:14-27

The next morning, David wrote a letter to Joab and sent it with Uriah. In the letter, he wrote:

'Put Uriah at the front of the fiercest fighting, then withdraw from him so that he is struck down and dies.'

When Joab was besieging the city, he put Uriah in the place where he knew the best enemy soldiers were. Then the men of the city came out and attacked Joab, and some of the men from David's soldiers fell in battle; Uriah the Hethite also died. Joab sent someone to report to David all the details of the battle. He commanded the messenger, "When you've finished telling the king all the details of the battle — if the king's anger gets stirred up and he asks you, 'Why did you get so close to the city to fight? Didn't you realize they would shoot from the top of the wall? At Thebez, who struck Abimelech son of Jerubbesheth? Didn't a woman drop an upper millstone on him from the top of the wall so that he died? Why did *you get so close to the wall?' — then say, 'Your servant Uriah the Hethite is dead also.'" Then the messenger left.*

*When he arrived, he reported to David all that Joab had sent him to tell. The messenger reported to David, "The men gained the advantage over us and came out against us in the field, but we counterattacked right up to the entrance of the city gate. However, the archers shot down on your servants from the top of the wall, and some of the king's servants died. Your servant Uriah the Hethite is also dead." David told the messenger, "Say this to Joab: 'Don't let this matter upset you because the sword devours all alike. Intensify your fight against the city and demolish it.' Encourage him." When Uriah's wife heard that her husband Uriah had died, she mourned for him. When the time of mourning ended, David had her brought to his house. She became his wife and bore him a son. However, the LORD considered what David had done to be evil."*

### Nathan's Parable and David's Repentance
### 2 Samuel 12:1-23

*"So the LORD sent Nathan to David. When he arrived, he said to him:*

*There were two men in a certain city, one rich and the other poor. The rich man had very large flocks and herds, but the poor man had nothing except one small ewe lamb that he had bought. He raised her, and she grew up with him and with his children. From his meager food she would eat, from his cup she would drink, and in his arms she would sleep. She was like a daughter to him. Now, a traveler came to the rich man, but the rich man could not bring himself to take one of his sheep or cattle to prepare for the traveler who had come to him. Instead, he took the poor man's lamb and prepared it for his guest.*

*David was infuriated with the man and said to Nathan: "As the LORD lives, the man who did this deserves to die! Because he has done this thing and shown no pity, he must pay four lambs for that lamb." Nathan replied to David, "You are the man! This is what the LORD God of Israel says: 'I anointed you king over Israel, and I rescued you from Saul. I gave your master's house to you and your master's wives into your arms, and I gave you the house of Israel and Judah, and if that was not enough, I would have given you even more. Why then have you despised the LORD's command by doing what I consider evil? You struck down Uriah the Hethite with the sword and took his wife as your own wife — you murdered him with the Ammonite's sword. Now therefore, the sword will never leave your house because you despised me and took the wife of Uriah the Hethite to be your own wife.' "This is what the LORD says, 'I am going to bring disaster on you from your own family: I will take your wives and give them to another before your very eyes, and he will sleep with them in broad daylight. You acted in secret, but I will do this before all Israel and in broad daylight.'" David responded to Nathan, "I have sinned against the LORD."*

*Then Nathan replied to David, "And the LORD has taken away your sin; you will not die. However, because you treated the LORD with such contempt in this matter, the son born to you will die." Then Nathan went home.*

*The LORD struck the baby that Uriah's wife had borne to David, and he became deathly ill. David pleaded with God for the boy. He fasted, went home, and spent the night lying on the ground. The elders of his house stood beside him to get him up from the ground, but he was unwilling and would not eat anything with them. On the seventh day, the baby died. But David's servants were afraid to tell him the baby was dead. They said, "Look, while the baby was alive, we spoke to him, and he wouldn't listen to us. So, how can we tell him the baby is dead? He may do something desperate." When David saw that his servants were whispering to each other, he guessed that the baby was dead. So, he asked his servants, "Is the baby dead?"*

*"He is dead," they replied. Then David got up from the ground. He washed, anointed himself, changed his clothes, went to the LORD's house, and worshiped. Then he went home and requested something to eat. So, they served him food, and he ate. His servants asked him, "Why have you done this? While the baby was alive, you fasted and wept, but when he died, you got up and ate food." He answered, "While the baby was alive, I fasted and wept because I thought, 'Who knows? The LORD may be gracious to me and let him live.' But now that he is dead, why should I fast? Can I bring him back again? I'll go to him, but he will never return to me."*

When I learned that the baby died, I could not stop crying, and I was so upset. How could God punish the baby for what his parents did? All I could think about was my sweet baby girl. Would she be punished for my sins? These questions tormented me so much that I couldn't leave the room without having some peace about what I just heard.

Brentwood Baptist does something that I love at the end of each service. "Next Steps" are the calls to action given before dismissing the congregation. "I don't know where you are in your journey, but before you leave, we'll be up at the front or the Next Steps banner to talk to you. Maybe you want to become a member of the church, want to join a life group, or need to talk to someone to help you walk through whatever storm you're in now. Don't leave this room until you do whatever that next step calls you to do."

So, I waited until there was a break in the line of people wanting to talk to him, and I nervously walked up to him, feeling guilty and holding my sweet baby. I told Aaron that the message today upset me. It hurt me so much to know that God punished David by taking the life of his infant son, and I was worried that God would punish me by taking out consequences on my infant. I believe my interpretation caught him off guard, and he was surprised to hear it. Nevertheless, Aaron made three points very clear to me.

1.) David was "God's guy," His appointed King. He was not just any human, and that's why the punishment for his severe crime was met with a severe response from God.

2.) Everyone is a sinner. Having a child out of wedlock is not a sin, calling for punishment as a result. (Having sex before marriage and without the faithful love and responsibility of a husband is a sin) God is a redeeming God, and being blessed with a baby is a miracle. That's why people don't get pregnant and carry babies to term every single time they have intercourse.

3.) This is not a surprise to God. Before I was born, God had a plan for me and knew that I would become Evelyn's mother, which also means He has a plan for her.

This means we are exactly where we are supposed to be right now.

*"For I know the plans I have for you," declares the Lord, "plans to prosper you and not to harm you, plans to give you hope and a future." – **Jeremiah 29:11***

This conversation brought me peace and confidence and cemented my connection to Brentwood Baptist as a church home for my daughter and me. I began taking her to the nursery in the children's ministry and started to draw closer to my budding relationship with Jesus.

# Begin Again 2013

*Unassuming Beginnings*

2013 started as an unassuming year for many of us. We were growing and expanding at Black River and in our family, but I don't think we knew the seeds being planted then. At the beginning of the year, a promising young female songwriter spent a lot of time at Black River and captivated the attention of our CEO, Gordon Kerr, and VP of Publishing, Celia Froehlig. I remember the day Gordon walked her around to all of the departments of Black River, introducing her to the staff. I was sitting with the promotion team when she came in with her guitar and played us a song in Bill Macky's office. She was poised, authentic, sweet as can be, real, and relatable. When she left the room, we were taking in the moment until Bill broke the silence and said, "Well, I don't know who that was, but I'd take her to radio right now!" We all laughed and agreed.

Not long afterward, Gordon and Celia signed that 19-year-old young songwriter named Kelsea Ballerini to a publishing deal at Black River Publishing.

*Stepping Forward*

Brentwood Baptist is huge on Next Steps, asking at the end of every service, "What's your Next Step?" It's a question I had thought about since we'd been attending and loving this church for nearly two years. I knew that I wanted to become a member of Brentwood Baptist, and a part of that process, aside from taking their PLACE class, which helps individuals discover their spiritual gifts and find their place, is baptism. I went through the regular steps in the Catholic church: baptism, 1st communion, and CCD classes (I even taught them for 2 years at one point!) I went through confirmation and graduated from a Catholic high school, but as I've mentioned, it never really sunk in for me until I became a mother and started attending this church. Therefore, I knew that with my newfound faith, I needed a newfound public profession that I chose and not just the next thing to do on my checklist. It also didn't hurt that I'd get a strongly encouraged glance from down the row whenever someone's baptism was shown at church, either in the moment or lovingly shared on the video screen. "I know, I know," I'd say. "I'm going to do it soon." And I did. On August 18th, 2013, with family and friends in the congregation, I was "dunked in the water," as Evie put it, by Aaron Bryant, and it was an incredible day and an excellent precursor to my next Next Step.

*Serious Dedication*

As much as I was being prompted to raise my daughter in the church, and for me to be baptized as an adult, I also knew I was being prompted to have Evie dedicated. Similar to the Catholic baptism, which we hadn't done because we were not going to a Catholic church, Evelyn's dedication service was held in the big church at Brentwood Baptist on October 20th, 2013, and was attended by family and friends in Nashville. Gordon read the Life Verse: Psalms 127:3-5 and Evie and loved ones surrounded me while she and several other preschoolers were prayed over and dedicated to Jesus. I cried; as a parent, it was a beautiful moment to publicly profess that I'd be raising my daughter in the church.

Afterward, we gathered in the hall for a reception and went for ice cream with the Kerrs.

### She's Not Mine

The difference between knowing that you're blessed and knowing that all we have is a gift from God is vast. I knew I was blessed to be Evie's mother from the beginning, but while she was still very young, I also realized that she was sent to me from God, and it was my job to be a good steward of the precious life He entrusted to me until I have to give her back. She's not mine, she's His, just as I am His. My daughter knows that I love her more than anything on Earth. She also knows that everything we have comes from God, that God gave us to each other, and so we love Jesus above all because, through Him, we can be together forever, with Him in Heaven.

There is a lot of peace in knowing I'm not in control of her life and don't own her. I'm here to love, protect, teach, and treasure the greatest gift I've ever been given until we are called home.

### The Gift of Christmas

Working with and being surrounded by beautiful Christian people who lead by example has many benefits, but one of my favorites is Christmas. We celebrate Christmas yearly by gathering together and sharing laughs, food, drinks, and music. It's easily one of my favorite times of the year. One of the added joys of the season for me is that since Evie was just a baby at the time of the first Black River Christmas party, she was my plus one and has been ever since. After all, this is her family, too.

The Christmas party in 2013 was one to remember for several reasons. Held in the beautiful Governor's Club clubhouse, there were endless lights, trees, candies, smiling faces, tasty food, laughter, and music. Inside a beautiful white tent awaited a gift that would change lives—including mine. It was at the Christmas party when a 20-year-old Kelsea Ballerini unwrapped and signed her record deal to Black River Entertainment. I filmed this magical moment with my sweet baby in tow, which lives on YouTube.

# GROWING IN FAITH, 2014

*My Jesus Year*

I love that with every new year comes a birthday party for Evie. Celebrating her birth is a fun and memorable way to reminisce on great memories as we create new ones. This year, we marked the occasion with a gathering at Black River Entertainment with family and friends. Even Katie returned to Nashville with her new boyfriend, Sawyer. We had cake, ice cream, funny faces for a photo backdrop, and much love to celebrate.

Having a child transformed my thinking around birthdays to a different perspective—a mother's. This is something I never considered before. Now, when I celebrate my birthday, I imagine what a mother may have been doing, thinking, and feeling in the days leading up to the birth of her third child. I know precisely what I was doing in the days before Evie's birth, and it all led me to this very moment in the present day.

*Introductions*

2014 was a year that held a lot of travel and introductions for me. I met several people that year who would continue to help me grow, learn, and love. Interestingly, several of those people lived on the other side of the country in Los Angeles yet still offered me encouragement and love that I didn't even know I needed. This was the year that we began introducing Kelsea and her music to people who lived there as well as in New York and to radio stations all across the country as she did a vast radio tour.

That year, my upcoming birthday was even more special because it was my 33rd birthday, and I had been waiting for my "Jesus Year" for a long time. Waking up on July 11th, 2014, I took an inventory of how I felt waking up to a new age, and it was the first year that I knew I had one specific goal. I wanted to spend my Jesus year learning more about the life of Jesus than I had ever learned before, and to do that meant I needed to read the Bible. The WHOLE Bible, that year. That was the goal, and I was on a mission. I ordered a "Knowing Jesus Study Bible" to be there in time for me to begin on my birthday, and I opened it up to the book of Genesis to start reading the Old Testament.

Thankfully, because I had begun spending more time in the Word, I think I was starting to hear that "still, small voice" more clearly, and with Evie learning how to talk and asking more questions, I was very thankful for the promptings from time to time leading me down the right path.

*Asking the Right Question*

Evie had been spending her days with Melissa and her family across the street from my sister's house for quite some time now, and the conversations in our home reflected that. She'd tell me stories at dinner and be silly, sharing her day with me. One particular week, many of her stories circled around Charles' dad or Ella's dad, so I instinctively knew I would get a "dad" question very soon.

At dinner a few nights later, Evie told me another funny story about someone's dad and then got quiet when she finished. She played with her food with the fork she held and asked, "So, where's my daddy?" I had just taken a bit of food, so I took my time to chew and think. Although I knew the time was coming, I didn't know what to say. I kept looking at her and took another bite to buy me some additional time. Then I remembered two things. My sister Jacky adopted her two children, which eventually comes with its own questions. She told me one day, "Always answer the question in the best and most honest way you can, and then stop. Don't offer additional information past what they ask you because they may not be ready for more details." Secondly, I remembered a book that I used to get me out of a precarious situation with a curious child during my pregnancy called All Kinds of Families! which mainly showcases children of different types of families, lovingly and creatively. Pulling from those two memories the Holy Spirit guided me to, I answered her.

"Well, honey. There are all kinds of families, and our family is you and me right now. But so many people love you. Let's see if we can count how many people love you!" And we did. We counted and counted until we just started laughing and continued with dinner.

Whew, there it was, round 1. To be continued.


*So Close Yet So Far*

When I think about all Evie's dad and his family are missing out on, it makes me feel sad for them. He doesn't know this, but I ran into his sister once with Evie. I did a lot of early online stalking of him and his family while I was pregnant. I looked up his parents, siblings, family photos, and contact info and emailed it to my sisters. If I ended up missing or dead one day, I wanted them to have a place to start looking for me. How sad is that? Anyway, because of this research, I knew his sister's name and what she looked like from photos online. One day, I was at Target in Brentwood, trying to find a face steamer. I had looked everywhere and came up empty-handed. Evie was about 2 or 3, and as I was pushing the shopping cart to the exit, a woman caught my attention. She looked like she was daydreaming, stocking shelves. I saw her, about 5'4", with short dirty-blond hair, and thought, "That looks like 'Gina'." I got a little closer and read her name tag; it was her.

I didn't know what to do. I just stared. "Hi!" She said in a super-friendly voice. "May I help you find anything?" "No, thanks," I answered. I don't know what came over me, but then I said, "Actually, I'm trying to find a face steamer." I knew they didn't have one, but I wanted to talk to her. The whole time she answered me, I continued holding on to Evie, almost petting her head.

"We don't carry one, but you may be able to find one at Bed Bath and Beyond."

I swear I don't even think she looked at Evie. I thanked her and then walked towards the check-out. It felt like I heard God speak to me as I walked away. "Well, now you know where she is." I didn't feel like I needed to tell her or say anything more. Can you imagine standing face to face with your niece, not knowing it was your own flesh and blood looking back at you?

And she was right, I did find that steamer and Bed Bath and Beyond.

*Lifts Me Up*

Something I've embraced for as long as I can remember is the art of "hand-me-downs." Growing up with older siblings, we would pass down clothes, toys, music, shoes, and whatever else we wanted to discard or had outgrown to a younger child. Periodically, when our family who owned the 2nd Time Around thrift store in Rapid City, SD would visit us, our Great Aunt Arlys or Aunt Bert would bring with them bags of clothes for us girls to fight over, ahem– I mean, to go through and it was always fun to find new treasures. When the news broke that I was expecting a baby girl, the "hand-me-downs" started flowing in, and God truly blessed us. We were loaded up from her convertible crib, baby changing table, other household furniture, and baby clothes, from burping cloths to high-end dresses! God was fulfilling his promise to make sure we had what we needed, and He did so in abundance.

Babies grow out of things so quickly that it wasn't long before I had the privilege to start giving away "Hand Me Downs" of my own. It felt so good and so natural to give these items away. By the time my tiny baby was ready for a toddler bed, it was hard to believe, but with successful potty training completed, I felt that she needed the ability to get in and out of bed easily. Knowing I wanted to give her crib away, God put one place on my heart, so I reached out to Aaron Bryant, the pastor at

Brentwood Baptist's church plant, The Church at Avenue South, and asked if they could use it. Aaron welcomed the donation and invited me to visit with him when I dropped it off.

*So, What's Your Story?*

Aaron had become familiar with our story before my baptism and wanted to check in with me to see how Ev and I were doing. I told him things were great, and Evie was about to turn four. Then Aaron shared more about what was happening with him and their new church plant. Then, he asked me a question that led me to write this book. Aaron asked me if I would ever consider telling my story to help others who may find themselves in a similar position to the one I was in about five years earlier. In an interesting foreshadowing to this moment, I told Aaron that I was recently asked to write a little bit of a letter to a friend of a friend who was in that exact moment, right now, and I shared with him the following note from my iPhone:

*Almost four years ago, I was living 2,000 miles from home, barely making ends meet, chasing my dream in Nashville, TN. Although I was where I wanted to be, it was hard, and I often didn't have enough money to buy groceries.*

*Approaching three years into a company, I had hit the ceiling and was barely making 30k a year. I was 29, single, and so wanted to meet the right guy. I thought I found him, and the next day, my mom died.*

*Devastated doesn't come close to how hard that news rocked my world. I clung to that guy to get me through the hardest part of losing my mom, and he was there for me even though he lived on the other side of the country.*

*About six months later, we called it off because it was too hard being apart.*

*The first Mother's Day without our mom was fast approaching when I went on a trip with my sisters. We mourned her, but it was nice to be together and remember her too.*

*The night I returned to Nashville, I spent time with a character from my past. We were never serious, and I hadn't seen him in at least a year. That night, my first Mother's Day without my mom, I got pregnant.*

*"Oh, my God. I'm pregnant," I thought. "I can't even take care of myself!" One of my first calls was to schedule an abortion. They told me I could get an appointment in five days or so, and I set a time.*

*I told him, and he freaked out and told me I couldn't have a baby. Several of my family and friends were like, "Dawn, it is okay if you don't have a baby. You need to take care of yourself."*

*Fast forward four years. The phrase I say more on any given day than my whole life combined to this point is, "I love you so much!" God opened up every possible door I could handle to this point. He provides for us through our faith in Him. I am now three years into my dream job at a record label. (YES! I had my second job interview the LAST Day I was pregnant!)*

*I have never made a better decision than to welcome this gift from God into my life, and I wouldn't be where I am or who I have been blessed to become without her. It's Unreal how much joy she brings me.*

*The guy has yet to meet her, and I don't know if he ever will. We don't need him because we have God, and we have the HUGE support system He's provided us from free medical during my pregnancy (I was poor) to childcare at the house across the street from my sister's now.*

*One day, I know God will also send her a daddy and me a husband, but right now, I am just so thankful for what we have because "What we have" is all I ever wanted and more than I could have known to wish for having.*

*I know I'm not you, and your situation is not mine. But God planned this for you before you were born, just like he did for my sweet girl and me. You can do this because it's already been written.*

*You can call me if you want to. I'm happy to listen.*

With that, I told him I'd absolutely be open to sharing my story whenever I could be of help.

The Hope Clinic in Nashville, TN, can be reached at (615) 321-0005. They are also ready to take calls.

# A SOLID FOUNDATION
## 2015

*Living a Dream*

When I turned 34, I woke up with a renewed feeling of peace, and I can't help but think it's because of the family God gave us in Nashville. How vital the Kerrs have been in our lives cannot be understated, from taking a chance on hiring me in the first place and being a huge and loving part of our daily culture to taking us under their spiritual wing and leading Evelyn and me to be baptized as followers of Jesus. I am so thankful for their friendship and for giving me an example of how to live a life of faith.

In 2015, my world grew a lot; we finally had success at work, and our company expanded. This was a special year for the Academy of Country Music as they celebrated their 50th anniversary of the ACM Awards, and they did it BIG, the only place you can, Texas. This was a special treat for me because my sister Kristy lived in Texas, and since I had to be in LA the following week for the Radio Disney Awards, she offered to keep Evie for me while I was working. My sister Stephanie wanted in on the fun, so she flew down to Dallas, piled into my hotel room with the three of us, and made a little family vacation out of it. As it turned out, some extra tickets would have otherwise gone unused, and I was able to have my sisters, my daughter, and my brother-in-law Andy join me to watch the awards show.

After having just been diagnosed with cancer, Taylor Swift's mom, Andrea, was on stage, giving a small speech before presenting an ACM award to her daughter. It was an incredible moment, and I choked up. I turned to look at my family, and it hit me. As special as the moment unfolding on stage was, I was literally realizing my dream in that very moment by being at the 50th ACM Awards – the year our artist Kelsea Ballerini's debut single "Love Me Like You Mean It" went No. 1 and she released her history-making debut album *The First Time*. All I could think about was how ridiculously proud my mother would have been for me at that moment, and then multiply that number by infinity because I was able to share that moment with my daughter, my sisters Stephanie and Kristy, and Kristy's husband, Andy. This was one of the first real moments when I thought to myself, " This is real. Thank you, God."

*Evie's New Prayer*

One of the greatest joys I find in parenting is seeing the good come out through my daughter's words or actions. I love seeing her respond to situations with faith or wisdom that cause me to sit back in awe and think to myself, whoa. I witnessed a moment like this one night when we were doing prayers. We do P.R.A.Y. as a way for each of us to walk through our day. First, we give Praise, Repent where we need to, Ask God for things we need His help with, or present our requests. Then, we Yield to what God tells us. On this particular night, Evelyn said,

"I would like to praise for my Mama and my daddy. Wait, I don't have a daddy."

Her prayer was so innocent, almost like a stream of consciousness, that it simultaneously moved me and broke my heart. It is important to me that my daughter can talk to me about anything, and talking about her not having a father at home is very important to discuss when she wants to because I never want her to feel like she lacks, even though our family is smaller than many other families are with both parents at home. The thing that is key for her, and frankly for me as well, is that we don't achieve wholeness or completeness by having another person in our lives. We are whole and perfectly loved as we are, the size we are, through Jesus Christ. A bigger family would be nice, but it's not essential to our peace and purpose.

I quickly jumped in and said, "Yes, you do, and he needs your prayers. Even though he's not with us right now, he is out there in the world, and it is okay to pray for him. I think it's good."

After that night, she gave "praise for her daddy" countless nights before closing her eyes and going to sleep.

*The Important Man*

One of the challenges I've faced as a parent is figuring out how to answer the tough questions about the world we live in posed to me by my sweet, innocent child. I believe that the city of Nashville and its citizens do great work in the struggle to provide for the least fortunate and the homeless. My daughter always notices when we pass someone struggling at an intersection or a stoplight.

"What does his sign say?" she would ask me before she could read. It's hard to read a sign to her that says, "Hungry. Anything helps. God bless." or one that says, "Single mom, needs work to feed my family" as we're driving past them with a carload of groceries or fast food.

"Why don't you help them?" She would ask me with a sad and curious heart. "Well, baby, I don't have any money on me. I only have a card." To try and ease her mind, I'd continue," We can't help everyone, but we do help where we can by giving to our church. When Mama gives the church money on Sundays, that money goes to help fund the work of God, which helps struggling people."

It's even harder when someone outright asks for help, like the night we were grabbing a quick dinner at Wendy's. As we started to drive away from the restaurant with our food, a man approached my car window.

"Do you have any spare change to help me out?" He asked. "No," I replied, "I'm sorry. I only have a card." Then he said, "I'm hungry. Would you buy me a hamburger?"

Knowing that I could buy him a hamburger and that I was about to set an example either way for my little one in the back seat, I agreed and asked him what he'd like to drink.

As we drove around a second time to place his order, Evelyn asked me what we were doing, and I explained it to her.

She replied," I want to give the Godly man his food." Curious, I asked her, "Why do you say he's a 'Godly man'?"

"Because he is." She stated, very matter-of-fact.

When we had his order in the car, I handed it to her so she could deliver it, as requested. He approached my window, and I nodded to the back seat.

"Here you go." She said with a smile.

"Thank you, little one," he said. "God Bless."

As we drove away, I heard a confident little voice in the back seat say, "Told ya."

My heart was full and humbled.

# OUR ROOTS – 2016

*The Grand Ole Opry*

When country music artists talk about the Grand Ole Opry, they often describe a kind of magic you can't quite put into words. I can't imagine how it would feel to stand in that sacred circle to sing, but I've been lucky enough to stand side-stage, backstage, and beside it. Watching people I love step into that circle from their debut, the fiftieth time, to the moment they become an Opry member. It *never* stops being special.

I remember my first time walking through the artist entrance to backstage at the Opry House. I had just passed the mail wall and was walking towards the lockers and I was face to face with Randy Owen, the lead singer of Alabama. He smiled and kept walking not knowing what was happening in my brain.

I was blown away because as a little girl, my parents LOVED Alabama. My first concert memory was me in a little Alabama T-shirt in line for their M&G before a summer show. I had my concert ticket in hand and when it was my turn to hand it so Randy to sign, I was so nervous that with a flick of my wrist, I slide it across the table to him. He laughed, threw his hands up like, "Ohhh, I'm so scary!" and happily signed it for me. By the end of that M&G, Jeff Cook was holding me and they jokingly asked if they could take me on the road with them.

Seeing Randy again, on that pivotal first time backstage at the Opry, felt very much like I was exactly where God wanted me to be.

I've been backstage during heartbreak, too, like after the 2010 flood in Nashville, when the circle was swept away along with so much of the Opry with it. When the day came to return the circle to center stage, the Opry house still looked gutted, missing the famous pews as the floor was being repaired. As I stood by and watched Brad Paisley and Little Jimmy Dickens during the intimate ceremony, a feeling of joy burst through the tears, and the circle was truly unbroken, and back where it belonged.

Years later, Evelyn came back to the Opry with me, but this time was different. We signed Bobby Bones and the Raging Idiots to the label, and in a fun twist, they recorded a kids album. Evelyn was among several other little ones to sing gang vocals on the *Raging Kidiots* album and is included in a couple of their music videos. That night in 2016, I stood side stage next to Dan Rogers. Opry Dan, as he is affectionately known in Nashville is now the Senior Vice President & Executive Producer of the Grand Ole Opry. Alongside Dan, Gina Keltner is another staple at the Opry. Both incredibly talented, kind and smart humans, I like to think of Dan and Gina as "Dad and Mom" of the Opry. They protect it and help the Opry thrive, with smiling faces and warm hearts.

As Bobby Bones and the Raging Kidiots, complete with gang vocals, were about to take the stage, Dan leaned over to me and said,

*"Is baby about to do something mama has never done before?"*

With the most proud and tearful disbelief nod, I chuckled in the affirmative.

Dan gave me one of his knowing, warm smiles and said,

*"Well, to be fair, your parents weren't movers and shakers in the music business."*

With that gracious acknowledgment, I watched as our proud little ones, my Evelyn, Tanya's Kalyn and Dawson, and Gina's Eden, marched out to a full Opry house to perform "When I Grow Up."

The Grand Ole Opry has always been more than a stage or a place. Our country music roots trace right back to the Opry, the longest-running radio program and a staple for any visit to Nashville. No wonder it's celebrating its 100th year in October 2025.

*"Hi Nana"*

When my daughter was five, things felt secure and sound overall. Making sure I had her in a great learning environment was paramount for me to try and give her the best start possible. She had just finished a Pre-K program that we loved, and I knew she was officially in an excellent school for kindergarten. I was relieved when we landed a ticket into the fantastic new school via the lottery system, thanks to an incredible friend who stood in line for me to register while I was on the road for work in Los Angeles. I knew we would be set for the next five years until it was time to move into the next school.

We've been blessed to make it home a few times for Easter, and this year was no exception, other than when we did it a little early at Grandma's house. Grandma T is my mom's mom, and since my mother passed away in 2009, she's meant even more to me than I can say (which reminds me, I should call her tonight; call yours too if you can!). When we visit Grandma, it's in the same house I used to listen for Santa's reindeer paws to hit the roof on Christmas Eve as a child. While we're there, we often visit mom too, at the cemetery on the edge of the small of McClusky, ND.

My daughter had never met my mom as she was born two years after my mom passed away, but it's beautiful to me how she still keeps my mom in her heart.

We had been standing in front of my mother's gravestone for a few minutes before she said a single sentence that brought me to tears yet again while typing it nearly ten years later. I'll never forget seeing Evelyn and my nephew Cooper standing there, five years old and adorable. When it was time to go, she crouched down and said to my mom, "Hi Nana, it's time for me to go now, but when I get to Heaven, I'm going to give you a big hug."

There's nothing like the pure love between a parent and their child.


*Flying and Memories of Mom*

Today I'm on my way to Las Vegas, NV, to meet our Sr. Director of Marketing Tanya Welch and crew to shoot a music video for Kelsea Ballerini's "Peter Pan." While on a layover in Atlanta, I took the opportunity to sign up for

TSA Pre-Check, as I had some time to spare. Once I completed that with more time to spare, I figured I'd grab a quick lunch before boarding the three-hour and fifty-minute flight. As I was sitting there eating my chicken salad, gluten-free pretzels, and red pepper hummus, a voice from the lady sitting behind me caught my attention.

*"Mom! You're not following my fingers, it's over there!" she said, pointing to the garbage can.*

As I watched her mom align herself towards the garbage can and then walk back to the seats adjacent to mine, I thought about my mom. This lady is so fortunate to have a mom around to travel with her. She wasn't being unkind to her mother, but I related to the frustration, as I had experienced it myself with my own mother, trying to teach her how to use Excel spreadsheets over the phone. Her mother's appearance reminded me of my mom when I saw her, with short, dark hair, glasses, and a similar stature.

This isn't the first time I've had an unexpected "mom" encounter at the airport. On one occasion, I was on the moving walkway between terminals in Minneapolis. As I stood still yet glided through the airport hallway, I studied the artwork as I passed by. Lining the wall leading into the Delta terminal were portraits drawn by local students.

As I casually looked on, one of the drawings made my heart skip a beat. It was my mom's face, to a T. The resemblance was uncanny. Her hair, glasses, and face stopped me in my moving tracks. So much so that I exited the moving walkway and retraced my steps to the portrait, snapping a photo on my iPhone. In shock, I sent the image to two of my sisters without a description. They immediately saw the resemblance and asked where I found that picture of our mom.

As my flight to Las Vegas drew nearer, I continued to people-watch and then boarded the plane. Thinking about work, praying for a safe return to my baby's arms, all of the usual thoughts I have on a plane. I'm an aisle person, an anxiety side effect from when I had that seizure in college, but since this flight is full, I swapped my assigned middle seat for a window seat a few rows away. It's always interesting to play the waiting game to see who will sit next to me on a flight when I'm traveling alone, which is most of the time. As I'm messing around on my phone and the flight is filling up, my row-mates approach, and there they were. The two ladies who caught my attention in the terminal were on my flight, and "mom" sat down next to me.

I thought, "It's not a big deal, I probably won't be affected again." About 20 minutes into the flight, but before takeoff, I realize her "mom" is wearing the same lotion my mom loved from Origins.

I thought, "Great, so now she even smells like her, lol." The mother-daughter duo got the giggles before taking off, and it made me smile because my sisters and I are notorious for the uncontrollable, unstoppable giggles.

Finally, we took off. I quietly wrapped up texting my work sister, Tanya, and sat in silence. Then the woman turns to me and speaks. Not the usual plane chatter, "Are you excited to go to Las Vegas?" or "Are you going on vacation or headed home?" No. She turns to me and, with a very sincere, familiar face, says,

*"Are you okay?"*

I was completely caught off guard. "Yes, thank you." I tried to convince myself she was asking if I was comfortable or had enough room, but I knew she wasn't.

And then I gathered courage and said, "Why do you ask?" Again, looking very sincere, she said,

*"Because you look sad."*

I lied and said, "My left eye is irritated from mascara or something being in it, but I'm fine."

Overwhelmed by how transparent I had been, apparently, I turned my head and began to silently cry. So I grabbed my phone, pulled my hair in front of my face to hide, and began to type this chapter.

I read once that we should be open to conversations with people because you never know when you're in the presence of an angel.

I'm not sure if she's an angel, but I'm thankful that my tears dried up, and I found the courage to tell her the truth and about my mom before the drink cart came out.


*The First Thing*

It was 2016 when the words of my pastor, Mike Glenn, hit their boiling point. Yes, I had reached a point in my life and career where things were feeling really good, yet I still wanted something more. I wanted the husband, the house, the dog, the yard, the boat, the lake cabin…these are still accurate now, but I'm going to stop myself because just typing it sounds very ungrateful.

"God won't give you the next thing until you do the first thing."

One night, I was caught up in thinking about all that I still wanted and all that I felt I was still missing in my life (see above list), and then I just said out loud, "It's okay, I have what I need." And just like that, I ANGERED my inner child.

"All you need. All you NEED?" My inner child screamed at me. "Dawn, you have an amazing, healthy, beautiful little girl, you work in the music industry – in your DREAM job, you live in a rent-controlled apartment in the most popular area of Nashville, YOU LIVE IN NASHVILLE, you are surrounded by incredible people that LOVE you and LOVE your daughter…ALL YOU NEED????

Okay, okay. Yes, I'm good. I'm sorry, me, inner me.

In February 2017, I received an email informing me that I reached another goal that I didn't even know to set. I was credentialed to work and attended the 2017 GRAMMY Awards with my Best New Artist nominee, Kelsea Ballerini, who also performed that evening. I legitimately cried when I received the email and felt honored and blessed.

"God won't give you the next thing until you do the first thing."

Shortly after that, I realized I am living beyond my greatest dreams, and it is my privilege, honor, and obligation to help others trust in God's plan for them to reach theirs, too.

Maybe I will add more blessings to my list of answered prayers, and if I do, it's out of the overflow of

God's goodness. We are blessed, loved, and completely whole, as we are, in His love. It is out of that love, and my best attempt at being obedient, to share my greatest solo, accompanied by God's grace, with you.

"God won't give you the next thing until you do the first thing."

# REDEMPTION

*There's More*

The awesome thing is that it wouldn't be the first and last time I received a letter confirming my credentials to go to the GRAMMY awards. I've worked the GRAMMYs five times now, and one of the highlights was watching our own Josh Kerr earn his first GRAMMY win for "God Only Knows," which he co-wrote and produced with for KING & COUNTRY, and the GRAMMY-winning version featuring Dolly Parton in 2020.

And isn't that the truth? God only knows what we've been through, and God only knows what incredible blessings he has waiting for us on the other side of our unbelief.

"Lord, I believe; help my unbelief!" Mark 9:24 NKJV

*Actual Forgiveness*

Listening to our pastor, Mike Glenn, always gives me a new perspective. One day in 2017, he got me good. See, I thought I had forgiven "Ben" for walking out my door in 2010 and never returning, that is, until I heard this from my pastor. "Forgiveness is releasing someone of the expectation that they will one day make it right." Forgiveness wipes it away like it never happened, so I can't forgive him while also expecting/hoping he will show up one day and make some kind of effort or admit fault. To truly forgive him, I have to actually let it go. Like the string of a balloon, once that sucker is up in the sky, I'm not getting it back. So, I wrote him a letter/text forgiving and releasing him.

## More Questions

The next time Evelyn asked me about her Father was when she was in the third grade. She had a couple of new friends come over from school to play at our apartment. They spent a lot of time in her room having fun while I was cooking dinner. Just before it was time for them to leave, they began to look at the many pictures of family and friends on our photo wall.

They spotted a photo of Ev and Jimmy and asked, "Is that your dad?" I listened intently as Evelyn nonchalantly replied with a simple "No." One of the girls followed up with the question, "Where are the pictures of your dad?" Again, Evelyn was relaxed and answered, "I don't have a dad." Confused, her friend replied, "Everyone has a dad." At that point, I chimed in with my "standard reply," "There are all kinds of families, and right our family is us two."

Once they left, I realized I should check in with Evelyn and see how she was doing. It had been a long time since we talked about him, so we sat on the couch and went for it.

I told her that I was proud of how well she answered questions from her friends, and I asked her if she had any questions for me to help her better navigate these conversations in the future. She said, "I want to know more about my dad. What's his name?"

I wasn't ready to say his name, so I said, "I'm not ready to tell you his name right now. Ask me something else."

She quickly followed up with, "What does he look like? What's his hair like?" as she raised her arms and motioned around her head with an excited smile. I answered those questions. "What's his name? I shook my head no. "How tall is he? Like, who does he compare to in height?" I answered her questions, and she asked me again, "What's his name?" Then I asked her, "Why do you want to know his name?" She said, "So I can find him and go talk to him." I asked her, "And what would you do or say when you find him?" She confidently said, "I would walk up to him and say, 'Hi, I'm Evelyn, I'm your daughter.'"

She is an incredibly smart, kind, and logical little lady. Evelyn's response suddenly jogged my memory and reminded me of something Dr. Laura said on her radio talk show one day. When talking to a caller about a father they had never met and felt rejected by, Dr. Laura stopped her mid-sentence with the brash yet loving tone she's known for. I'm paraphrasing, but essentially, she said, "You can't be rejected by someone who has never met you. He has never met YOU; he doesn't know YOU. His choice is not something that YOU should take personally because it has NOTHING to do with YOU." That gave me great confidence in one day utilizing that little piece of information to help Evelyn as she continues to grow up without a father. I guess that day is today.

My goal was to explain to her that even though he's not her dad and not in her life, it's not a reflection of her.

It's not because of who she is that he's never met her. It's because of who HE is. He doesn't know her to reject her. So, I decided to make my point through an analogy to explain to her how I think about her situation. (Side note: I HATE that word, situation, in this context as it was used in describing my "situation" as an unwed mother. So why keep it in this book? Because I think it should be outed as the insensitive and unloving word it is in hopes that maybe someone will think twice before saying it to or about someone who finds themselves in similar circumstances that I found myself initially terrified in all those years ago and am thriving in today.)

Anyway, this example is very close to home to her and perhaps might be helpful to someone else.

Two of Evelyn's cousins are adopted. They have all grown up close together, and it's always been open and celebrated that they were adopted. So, I told her, "Sometimes, when people find out they're going to be parents, they are so excited! They can't wait to be a parent and immediately begin planning and preparing for the baby. Other times, they are not ready to be a parent for whatever reason in their own life. They know that they can't do what's best for the child as their parent, so they let someone else be their parent."

She nodded, and I continued. "That's how your cousins became part of our family. They were adopted because their birth parents knew that they couldn't give them the lives they wanted for them, so they let Auntie Jackie and Uncle David be their parents."

I continued as she listened intently. "When I found out that I was going to be a mom, at first I was scared, but once I trusted God's plan for us, I was so excited! I couldn't wait to meet you, and love you! But when I told him that he would be a dad, he knew that he wasn't ready and he wasn't in a place in his life where he could be a good father. So, he gave his part of parenting up to me, kind of like an adoption does. So, I'm holding his part, and I'm holding my part as your mom. One day, if I get married, I'll hand that piece over to my husband, who will adopt you and be your Father. But right now, I'm holding both pieces, and that's our family, and it is good."

She understood, and it's brought us much peace ever since.

She asked me one last time for his name. I thought she deserved to know it, so I told her his name. His full name. She laughed, saying she liked our last name better than his, a much longer Italian last name. And that was it. She's never seen a picture of what he looks like and hasn't asked about him much since.

# THE GREATEST IS LOVE



*Joy in Sadness*

Nearing the end of my 30s, like the end of my 20s, brought immense sadness. In July of 2019, about 20 minutes after my sister Stephanie and her family returned home early from a two-week vacation visiting family in Florida, my dad had a stroke, sitting on the couch right next to my sister. Being the astute nurse she is, she noticed the signs as they unfolded and had him in the ER in less than 20 min. She did everything right, but we often thought we would lose him. I flew up there on my birthday and saw him in the ICU in the worst, unresponsive form I have ever seen my Father. Selfishly, I prayed and begged God not to take him home on my birthday. My siblings and I agreed to have my dad transferred to the hospital in Bismarck, where my sister could keep a better eye on him. In Fargo, they were talking palliative care, and really, there wouldn't have been family there to stay with him. Remarkably, he spent almost 30 days in the hospital, and by the time he left, he was walking with the help of a walker.

After several months of rehab and significant progress, Dad was home and doing very well, considering where the stroke left him. He was walking without help around the house, up and down stairs, and talking well for the most part. His swearing was impeccable, even at the hospital. I think that, combined with his utter stubbornness and wit, got him through those darker days.

I was home for Christmas that year; thankfully, we were able to spend a lot of time together. Dad had been to Nashville a couple of years before all this happened, and we had an incredible trip; we even went to an NFL Tennessee Titans football game with my sister Jacky. It was a blessing that he could see more of our life since so much had changed since my early days in Nashville.

Eight months later, on March 13th, Steph was taking my dad to the airport to see my youngest sister before she flew to Texas, and he collapsed in the driveway. Dad went to Heaven that day, and I got a call shortly afterward.

This time, Steph called me. I knew she was taking him to the airport, so I half expected her to call and report how it went.

"We didn't make it to the airport," she said.

I understood; he's 83, and it's cold outside. I thought she meant the stayed in the warm house and missed getting there.

"Dad died," she said. And she started to cry. I began to cry, and then we called Kristy together.

I forgot how much this hurts. Suddenly, I'm back to that feeling from 10 years ago of being unable to breathe. There was a significant difference this time, though.

After I hung up the phone, Ev snuggled in beside me and asked what was wrong. I told her about Papa, and she was sad to hear it. Without missing a beat, she said,

*"Well, you know you're going to see him again, right?"*

I laughed, smiled, and gave her a big hug.

*"Yes, honey, I do."*

Then she said, *"I'm hungry. Will you make me some pancakes?"*

I smiled, kissed her little forehead, and made pancakes.

## Tag Team

I often receive compliments on being a good mother, and sometimes I'm asked, "How do you do it all?"

Being Evie's Mama is the second greatest gift I've ever received, and it is usually my automatic response (the first being Jesus sacrificing himself in my place so I can spend eternity with Him, the Father, and her up in Heaven). It's been her and me from the beginning of our life together, and that consistency helps with everything. We don't have the drama and fighting that comes with two parents who hate each other and still have to interact for the sake of a child. There are no custody issues, no child support fights (or hate mail, as I imagine a child support payment would contain between the zeros), no let-down hearts because he didn't pick her up for a weekend visit, or worse, him deciding to stop being involved at all and "peacing out" after she's already become accustomed to having a dad. We are free of that because we don't rely on him to provide emotional, physical, or financial support. We rely on God to provide for us, and He has done so in spades, whatever that expression means.

That said, it's not always easy. Days get long, and tempers get short. When we come home from a long day, and we're both tired, Evie listens to me much less than I'd like her to sometimes, and I can feel my blood pressure rising. Those are the moments where I wish I could tag someone into the round. "Go help your daughter get ready for bed, and I need a moment to myself to wind down." That's a statement I have yet to say out loud because there is no one to tag in. So, instead of my partner jumping in the ropes, I ask Jesus to jump in, usually out loud, because I need to hear it, too. Most times, I can tap into enough grace to get through bedtime without any issues, but sometimes, I can't. Sometimes, I'm mortified to admit it, but I lose my temper and yell. It's just the worst feeling. She's a little kid, and I'm shaping her life and memories, and I just yelled at her. She would usually cry and finally do what I asked of her, and we move on without another issue. Except that I'd feel terrible because I lost my temper, and she'd feel sad.

There is a rainbow after that storm, though. When I am wrong and know it, I have no choice but to tell her and ask her to forgive me. I can't tell you the last person I asked to forgive me, excluding Evie. I don't think people do that anymore. Even though I hate that I did something that required me to ask her to forgive me, I love that because I've led by example in doing so that she, too, asks for forgiveness when she messes up.

The brutal truth is I have failed, HARD. I accidentally sent out a press invite to the entire Nashville media industry with a curse word in the email's subject line! I've made bad choices with relationships. I've lost my patience and hurt the feelings of people I love. Nonetheless, I know I have been forgiven for these failures and many more. I know He forgives me, and I work every day to forgive myself and live for a better future.

God provides for us and continues to ensure we thrive every day. From successes at work to my happy and healthy horse-riding daughter, even that house I was whining about above. If we let Him, God turns our messes and heartbreak into His masterpiece.

Even though this journey is not all fun and games with smooth sailing, I know that the rough waters will be weathered with forgiving and gracious hearts.

*Right Where We're Supposed To Be*

It's incredible how fast time can fly, and how slowly a day can go by. I started writing this book on airplanes during work trips, a little bit at a time, in the Notes app on my phone. Sometimes I'd go days or months between adding to it. In that time, Evelyn has grown into a smart, funny, goofy, wise, and beautiful young lady. She started high school, yet she still has her childlike sparkle, and I'm so blessed and PROUD to be her mom.

Evelyn is getting baptized in a couple of weeks. It's such a beautiful next step in our journey together. We're still the mother/daughter duo, it's the two of us. And while love may come into my life, or maybe it won't, I know this: our little family is exactly what it's meant to be, right now. We've got our horse, our two dogs, and by the grace of God, we're good.

My Grandma T passed away since this book went into editing. I am happy to say that I sent her the draft to read years before and she loved it. I'm even happier to say that the year before she passed, my Aunt Marilyn and

Gram came to Tennessee to visit us on their way down to Mississippi and Gram got to witness our life.

She came to Black River and met my people, my Nashville family. Gordon gave her the honor of being the first person to turn on the newly installed neon light that reads, "Black River," in a cool blue light. Gram came to the barn and met Ev's horse, even grooming him, something she's never done before!

Having her in our home for those few days were some of the most precious moments of my life. I hope she had a lot of great things to report back to my parents. We are blessed, and ok.

I want to end with a little piece of wisdom that my grandmother added to a well-known Bible verse. I found one of her old *Jesus Calling* devotionals, and I think of this often.

*"This is the day the Lord has made; let us rejoice and be glad."* And then Gram added the simple, "**with help**."

It's that last part, "**with help**," that always stuck with me. Because no matter how strong we are or how much we carry, we all need help, and He is right there to give it to us.

So if this book finds you, I hope it's at the right time and that it helps.

# YOU TELL ME: THE FINAL CHAPTER?

Evelyn was born on January 29th. My mom passed away on November 29th. Writing that sentence all these years later, I still can't believe it. My mom's birthday and Mother's Day are in May. Evelyn was conceived on Mother's Day, the first one since I lost my mom; it's because of all those reasons I named Evelyn May after her Nana. God has blessed me even more than I could begin describing. The phrase I say the most every day is, "I love you." Everything about my life has been better since Evelyn came into it. Every. Single. Detail. God is in charge, and I put my complete faith and trust in him when I said yes to this miracle of her life. I couldn't have planned or dreamed things would work out better than they have, and that is why my faith journey starts with Evelyn. Saying yes to her was step one for me in my relationship with God. I know we are so blessed and perfectly provided for through Him. Thank you, Lord God. In Jesus name, I pray. Amen.

**Why am I writing this book? There are two main reasons, and God has given me both directives.**

Our pastor, Mike Glenn, told us a story about his friend living out his ministry in South Africa. He was a missionary down there, and it was very successful. His friend got sick a few years back, and although boarding a flight to South Africa was never something Mike thought he'd ever do, he knew he needed to.

I believe his friend answered the door and shut it in Mike's face out of disbelief. They began to talk when he opened it again and welcomed him into his home. Mike asked him, why did you stay here so long and expand your ministry?

His answer surprised him. He said, *"Matthew 25 scared me to death. I could just see myself standing in front of Jesus, and Jesus saying to me, 'John, you did well with that little church I gave you, but what about the thousands of people who are dying in Masiphumelele across the street?'"*

My first reason for writing this book is YOU. I feel like every day that passes without someone being able to learn about my story is a day that someone could be slipping through the cracks. Someone that our story could encourage. That encouragement could lead to a woman deciding to carry her baby to term and become a mother or bless another woman with motherhood. She could read about the peace God gave me and see the beauty of His blessings unfold, all because I said yes to His plan.

The second reason is simple: I believe God is not done with our story. There is more to come for us – blessings He has planned for us that stretch beyond my imagination. The responsibility that comes with being blessed is also to be a good steward of those blessings. I believe that to truly be a good steward of the life God has given us, it is my calling to tell everyone and anyone I can that they can be blessed, too, regardless of where they are right now. God works with us wherever we are.

All I've ever needed was Jesus, and he's all we need to live a blessed life filled with more love, support, and security than we could have ever dreamed of having. That's all anyone needs. At church one day, Mike said, "God will never give you more than you can handle." I've ALWAYS interpreted that to mean bad things. We can always get through our struggles if we keep our faith, but I didn't realize it meant blessings, too. I would have messed up a marriage if it came before I was ready. Once I share what I've learned and release this book into the world, it will genuinely be "My Greatest Solo, Accompanied by Grace." Then, I believe God will continue to grow our family and maybe yours, too.

**God won't tell you the next thing until you do the first thing**.

Most of the time, we already know what the first thing is. That's the funny and sometimes frustrating part of it all. That "still small voice" in our head/heart/gut is the Holy Spirit prompting us. Softly but firmly revealing the next, or perhaps first step. Maybe you haven't opened your heart up yet to let Jesus in, or you haven't joined a church to live life with as a part of Christ's family. Or maybe you haven't let go of your fears and simply said, "Yes, Jesus, I trust in you," when He calls on you to walk a path you never expected. Whatever it is, follow that divine guidance to your next step, and it will lead you to faith, hope, and, the greatest of all, love.

# Verses to Live By

*"See, I have engraved you on the palms of my hands; your walls are ever before me."* – **Isaiah 49:16**

*"Trust in the Lord with all your heart and lean not on your own understanding; in all your ways submit to him, and he will make your paths straight."*
– **Proverbs 3:5–6**

*"For I know the plans I have for you," declares the Lord, "plans to prosper you and not to harm you, plans to give you hope and a future."* – **Jeremiah 29:11**

*"For God so loved the world that he gave his one and only Son, that whoever believes in him shall not perish but have eternal life."* – **John 3:16**

*"If you declare with your mouth, 'Jesus is Lord,' and believe in your heart that God raised him from the dead, you will be saved."* – **Romans 10:9**

*"Everyone who calls on the name of the Lord will be saved."*
– **Romans 10:13**